fresh
from the sea

fresh
from the sea

Kate Whiteman

southwater

This edition is published by Southwater

Distributed in the UK by
The Manning Partnership
251-253 London Road East
Batheaston, Bath BA1 7RL
tel. 01225 852 727
fax 01225 852 852

Published in the USA by
Anness Publishing Inc.
27 West 20th Street
Suite 504
New York NY 10011
fax 212 807 6813

Distributed in Canada by
General Publishing
895 Don Mills Road
400-402 Park Centre
Toronto, Ontario M3C 1W3
tel. 416 445 3333
fax 416 445 5991

Distributed in Australia by
Sandstone Publishing
Unit 1, 360 Norton Street
Leichhardt
New South Wales 2040
tel. 02 9560 7888
fax 02 9560 7488

Southwater is an imprint of
Anness Publishing Limited
Hermes House
88-89 Blackfriars Road
London SE1 8HA
tel. 020 7401 2077
fax 020 7633 9499

© 2001 Anness Publishing Limited
Previously published as part of a larger compendium
The World Encyclopedia of Fish and Shellfish

1 3 5 7 9 10 8 6 4 2

Publisher: Joanna Lorenz
Executive Editor: Linda Fraser
Project Editor: Susannah Blake
Designer: Nigel Partridge
Photography: William Lingwood, assisted by Vanessa Davies
Food for Photography: Sunil Vijayakar, assisted by Tonia Hedley

NOTES

For all recipes, quantities are given in both metric and imperial measures and, where appropriate, measures
are also given in standard cups and spoons. Bracketed terms are intended for American readers.
Follow one set, but not a mixture, because they are not interchangeable.

Standard spoon and cup measures are level.

1 tsp = 5ml, 1 tbsp = 15ml, 1 cup = 250ml/8fl oz

Australian standard tablespoons are 20ml. Australian readers should use 3 tsp in
place of 1 tbsp for measuring small quantities of gelatine, cornflour, salt etc.

Medium (US large) eggs are used unless otherwise stated.

CONTENTS

INTRODUCTION

Fish is an extremely versatile food and there are any number of delicious ways to cook it. It is only worth having, however, if it is absolutely fresh. Look for fish that has shiny skin with a metallic glint. The eyes should be clear, bright and slightly bulging. The flesh should feel firm and springy when you press it lightly with your finger. Look for a firm tail and plentiful, shiny, close-fitting scales.

When buying fish, shop with an open mind; be prepared to purchase whatever looks freshest and best on the day, then build your menu around it. If you don't have a good fishmonger you might be buying your fish from a supermarket. If so, make sure that ready-prepared white fish fillets, steaks and cutlets are neatly trimmed, with moist, firm, translucent flesh.

If you are buying frozen fish make sure it comes from a reputable store with a quick turnover. Transport your fish home as quickly as possible and put it straight into the freezer. Commercially frozen fish is often frozen on the ships that catch it, and at temperatures well below the average domestic freezer to preserve the delicate texture of the flesh, so although fresh fish is best, properly frozen fish is a reasonable alternative.

When discussing shellfish it is impossible to divorce preparation and cooking techniques, since one is bound up so closely with the other. Lobsters and crabs are cooked live, for instance; mussels are opened and cooked in one simple process. Crustaceans and molluscs need very little cooking to enhance their already superb flavour. In

Above: Baking a whole fish is incredibly easy. This snapper is cooked with chilli and coconut milk, and only needs plain boiled rice and to accompany it.

Below: Moules Provençales is a classic way of cooking mussels with bacon and white wine. The dish can be served as a starter or as a light lunch.

Below: Fresh trout make a delicious supper that is easy to prepare, just grill them with butter and serve with lemon.

Above: These beautifully fresh whitebait can be deep fried into cripsy morsels and eaten with brown bread and lemon.

fact, many molluscs can be eaten raw, provided they are extremely fresh and come from unpolluted waters.

Many of the methods used for cooking fish are suitable for shellfish, particularly poaching, frying, grilling and steaming. Almost any cooking method suits fish except boiling. Because fish is so delicate it is always better to

undercook rather than overcook it. Take fish out of the fridge at least 30 minutes before cooking so that it cooks evenly.

The recipes in this book use a wide variety of fish, including conger eel, lobster, clams, halibut, turbot, salt cod, and many more. The dishes take their inspiration from around the world, using the flavours of many cuisines, and they

Above: Oysters Rockefeller are a perfect way of lightly cooking shellfish; the spicy, tangy stuffing perfectly complementing the soft, salty oyster.

range from simple to more complex dishes. Warm Swordfish and Rocket Salad, for example, or Smoked Mackerel Pâté take just minutes to prepare, while more elaborate dishes such as terrines and Bouillabaisse take a bit longer, but are well worth the effort. If your taste tends towards oriental flavours you might want to try Aromatic Tiger Prawns or Thai Fish Broth, or it might be the time of year where you long for creamy fish dishes to warm and sustain you, such as indulgent Fish Pie, luscious Seafood Lasagne or rich Lobster Ravioli.

Whether you want to bake a whole fish, flash-fry some delicate fillets, or go for a full scale entertaining extraganza with Lobster Thermidor, this book will supply you with every fish recipe you could possibly need.

Left: A terrine, such as this one made from haddock and smoked salmon, is a perfect dinner party dish that can be cooked well in advance.

SOUPS

From light, spicy broths to hearty one-pot meals, fish and shellfish soups

are a delight. Chilled Cucumber and Prawn Soup is perfect for

summer eating, while Scallop and Jerusalem Artichoke Soup and

substantial Bouillabaisse make wonderful winter warmers along with

Clam Chowder from New England. For real luxury,

treat yourself and your guests to creamy Lobster Bisque, or travel to

Asia with spicy Malaysian Prawn Laksa and the

wonderfully fragrant Thai Fish Broth.

CHILLED CUCUMBER AND PRAWN SOUP

If you've never served a chilled soup before, this is the one to try. Delicious and light, it's the perfect way to celebrate summer.

SERVES FOUR

INGREDIENTS
25g/1oz/2 tbsp butter
2 shallots, finely chopped
2 garlic cloves, crushed
1 cucumber, peeled, seeded
  and diced
300ml/½ pint/1¼ cups milk
225g/8oz/2 cups cooked peeled
  prawns (shrimp)
15ml/1 tbsp each finely chopped
  fresh mint, dill, chives and chervil
300ml/½ pint/1¼ cups
  whipping cream
salt and ground white pepper
For the garnish
  30ml/2 tbsp crème fraîche (optional)
  4 large, cooked prawns (shrimp),
    peeled with tail intact
  fresh dill and chives

2 Stir in the milk, bring almost to boiling point, then lower the heat and simmer for 5 minutes. Tip the soup into a blender or food processor and process until very smooth. Season to taste.

3 Pour the soup into a large bowl and leave to cool. When cool, stir in the prawns, chopped herbs and cream. Cover, transfer to the refrigerator and chill for at least 2 hours.

4 To serve, ladle the soup into four individual bowls and top each portion with a spoonful of crème fraîche, if using, and place a prawn over the edge of each dish. Sprinkle a little extra chopped dill over each bowl of soup and tuck two or three chives under the prawns on the edge of the bowls to garnish. Serve immediately.

1 Melt the butter in a pan and cook the shallots and garlic over a low heat until soft but not coloured. Add the cucumber and cook gently, stirring frequently, until tender.

COOK'S TIP
If you prefer hot soup, reheat it gently until hot but not boiling. Do not boil, or the delicate flavour will be spoilt.

VARIATION
If you like, you can use other cooked shellfish in place of the peeled prawns – try fresh, frozen or canned crab meat, or cooked, flaked salmon fillet.

SCALLOP AND JERUSALEM ARTICHOKE SOUP

THE SUBTLE SWEETNESS OF SCALLOPS COMBINES WELL WITH THE FLAVOUR OF JERUSALEM ARTICHOKES IN THIS ATTRACTIVE GOLDEN SOUP. FOR AN EVEN MORE COLOURFUL VERSION, SUBSTITUTE PUMPKIN FOR THE ARTICHOKES AND USE EXTRA STOCK INSTEAD OF THE MILK.

SERVES SIX

INGREDIENTS

1kg/2¼lb Jerusalem artichokes
juice of ½ lemon
115g/4oz/½ cup butter
1 onion, finely chopped
600ml/1 pint/2½ cups fish stock
300ml/½ pint/1¼ cups milk
generous pinch of saffron threads
6 large or 12 small scallops, with
 their corals
150ml/¼ pint/⅔ cup
 whipping cream
salt and ground white pepper
45ml/3 tbsp flaked (sliced) almonds
 and 15ml/1 tbsp finely chopped
 fresh chervil, to garnish

1 Working quickly, scrub and peel the Jerusalem artichokes, cut them into 2cm/¾in chunks and drop them into a bowl of cold water, which has been acidulated with the lemon juice. This will prevent the artichokes from discolouring.

2 Melt half the butter in a pan, add the onion and cook over a low heat until softened. Drain the artichokes and add them to the pan. Cook gently for 5 minutes, stirring frequently. Pour in the stock and milk, add the saffron and bring to the boil. Lower the heat and simmer until the artichokes are tender but not mushy.

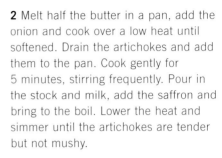

3 Meanwhile, carefully separate the scallop corals from the white flesh. Prick the corals and slice each scallop in half horizontally. Heat half the remaining butter in a frying pan, add the scallops and corals and cook very briefly (for about 1 minute) on each side. Dice the scallops and corals, keeping them separate, and set them aside until needed.

4 When the artichokes are cooked, tip the contents of the pan into a blender or food processor. Add half the white scallop meat and process until very smooth. Return the soup to the clean pan, season with salt and white pepper and keep hot over a low heat while you prepare the garnish.

5 Heat the remaining butter in a frying pan, add the almonds and toss over a medium heat until golden brown. Add the diced corals and cook for about 30 seconds. Stir the cream into the soup and add the remaining diced white scallop meat. Ladle the soup into individual bowls and garnish each serving with the almonds, scallop corals and a sprinkling of chervil.

MATELOTE

TRADITIONALLY THIS FISHERMEN'S CHUNKY SOUP INCLUDES CONGER EEL, BUT ANY FIRM FISH CAN BE USED. IF YOU CAN FIND IT DO INCLUDE AT LEAST SOME EEL, AND USE A ROBUST DRY WHITE OR RED WINE FOR EXTRA FLAVOUR.

SERVES SIX

INGREDIENTS

 1kg/2¼lb mixed fish, including
  450g/1lb conger eel if possible
 50g/2oz/¼ cup butter
 1 onion, thickly sliced
 2 celery sticks, thickly sliced
 2 carrots, thickly sliced
 1 bottle dry white or red wine
 1 fresh bouquet garni containing
  parsley, bay leaf and chervil
 2 cloves
 6 black peppercorns
 beurre manié for thickening, see
  Cook's Tip
 salt and cayenne pepper
For the garnish
 25g/1oz/2 tbsp butter
 12 baby (pearl) onions, peeled
 12 button (white) mushrooms
 chopped flat leaf parsley

1 Cut all the fish into thick slices, removing any obvious bones. Melt the butter in a large pan, put in the fish and sliced vegetables and stir over a medium heat until lightly browned. Pour in the wine and enough cold water to cover. Add the bouquet garni and spices and season. Bring to the boil, lower the heat and simmer gently for 20–30 minutes, until the fish is tender, skimming the surface occasionally.

2 Meanwhile, prepare the garnish. Heat the butter in a deep frying pan and sauté the baby onions until golden and tender. Add the mushrooms and fry until golden. Season and keep hot.

3 Strain the soup through a large strainer into a clean pan. Discard the herbs and spices in the strainer, then divide the fish among deep soup plates (you can skin the fish if you wish, but this is not essential) and keep hot.

4 Reheat the soup until it boils. Lower the heat and whisk in the *beurre manié*, little by little, until the soup thickens. Season it and pour over the fish. Garnish each portion with the fried baby onions and mushrooms and sprinkle with chopped parsley.

COOK'S TIP
To make the *beurre manié* for thickening, mix 15g/½oz/1 tbsp softened butter with 15ml/1 tbsp plain (all-purpose) flour. Add to the boiling soup a pinch at a time, whisking constantly.

FISH SOUP WITH ROUILLE

MAKING THIS SOUP IS SIMPLICITY ITSELF, YET THE FLAVOUR SUGGESTS IT IS THE PRODUCT OF PAINSTAKING PREPARATION AND COOKING.

SERVES SIX

INGREDIENTS

1kg/2¼lb mixed fish
30ml/2 tbsp olive oil
1 onion, chopped
1 carrot, chopped
1 leek, chopped
2 large ripe tomatoes, chopped
1 red (bell) pepper, seeded
  and chopped
2 garlic cloves, peeled
150g/5oz/⅔ cup tomato purée (paste)
1 large fresh bouquet garni,
  containing 3 parsley sprigs, 3 celery
  sticks and 3 bay leaves
300ml/½ pint/1¼ cups white wine
salt and ground black pepper

For the rouille

2 garlic cloves, roughly chopped
5ml/1 tsp coarse salt
1 thick slice of white bread, crust
  removed, soaked in water and
  squeezed dry
1 fresh red chilli, seeded and
  roughly chopped
45ml/3 tbsp olive oil
salt and cayenne pepper

For the garnish

12 slices of baguette, toasted in
  the oven
50g/2oz/½ cup finely grated
  Gruyère cheese

1 Cut the fish into 7.5cm/3in chunks, removing any obvious bones. Heat the oil in a large pan, then add the fish and chopped vegetables. Stir until these begin to colour.

2 Add all the other soup ingredients, then pour in just enough cold water to cover the mixture. Season well and bring to just below boiling point, then lower the heat to a bare simmer, cover and cook for 1 hour.

3 Meanwhile, make the rouille. Put the garlic and coarse salt in a mortar and crush to a paste with a pestle. Add the soaked bread and chilli and pound until smooth, or process in a food processor. Whisk in the olive oil, a drop at a time, to make a smooth, shiny sauce that resembles mayonnaise. Season with salt and add a pinch of cayenne if you like a fiery taste. Set the rouille aside.

4 Lift out and discard the bouquet garni from the soup. Process the soup in batches in a food processor, then strain through a fine strainer placed over a clean pan, pushing the solids through with the back of a ladle.

5 Reheat the soup without letting it boil. Check the seasoning and ladle into individual bowls. Top each serving with two slices of toasted baguette, a spoonful of rouille and some grated Gruyère.

COOK'S TIP
Any firm fish can be used for this recipe. If you use whole fish, include the heads, which enhance the flavour of the soup.

LOBSTER BISQUE

BISQUE IS A LUXURIOUS, VELVETY SOUP, WHICH CAN BE MADE WITH ANY CRUSTACEANS.

SERVES SIX

INGREDIENTS
  500g/1¼lb fresh lobster
  75g/3oz/6 tbsp butter
  1 onion, chopped
  1 carrot, diced
  1 celery stick, diced
  45ml/3 tbsp brandy, plus extra for
    serving (optional)
  250ml/8fl oz/1 cup dry white wine
  1 litre/1¾ pints/4 cups fish stock
  15ml/1 tbsp tomato purée (paste)
  75g/3oz/scant ½ cup long grain rice
  1 fresh bouquet garni
  150ml/¼ pint/⅔ cup double (heavy)
    cream, plus extra to garnish
  salt, ground white pepper and
    cayenne pepper

1 Cut the lobster into pieces. Melt half the butter in a large pan, add the vegetables and cook over a low heat until soft. Put in the lobster and stir until the shell on each piece turns red.

2 Pour over the brandy and set it alight. When the flames die down, add the wine and boil until reduced by half. Pour in the fish stock and simmer for 2–3 minutes. Remove the lobster.

3 Stir in the tomato purée and rice, add the bouquet garni and cook until the rice is tender. Meanwhile, remove the lobster meat from the shell and return the shells to the pan. Dice the lobster meat and set it aside.

COOK'S TIP
It is best to buy a live lobster, chilling it in the freezer until it is comatose and then killing it just before cooking. If you can't face the procedure, use a cooked lobster; take care not to over-cook the flesh. Stir for only 30–60 seconds.

4 When the rice is cooked, discard all the larger pieces of shell. Tip the mixture into a blender or food processor and process to a purée. Press the purée through a fine strainer placed over the clean pan. Stir the mixture, then heat until almost boiling. Season with salt, pepper and cayenne, then lower the heat and stir in the cream. Dice the remaining butter and whisk it into the bisque. Add the diced lobster meat and serve immediately. If you like, pour a small spoonful of brandy into each soup bowl and swirl in a little extra cream.

BOUILLABAISSE

AUTHENTIC BOUILLABAISSE COMES FROM THE SOUTH OF FRANCE AND INCLUDES RASCASSE (SCORPION FISH) AS AN ESSENTIAL INGREDIENT. IT IS, HOWEVER, PERFECTLY POSSIBLE TO MAKE THIS WONDERFUL MAIN-COURSE SOUP WITHOUT IT. USE AS LARGE A VARIETY OF FISH AS YOU CAN.

SERVES FOUR

INGREDIENTS
   45ml/3 tbsp olive oil
   2 onions, chopped
   2 leeks, white parts only, chopped
   4 garlic cloves, chopped
   450g/1lb ripe tomatoes, peeled
      and chopped
   3 litres/5 pints/12 cups boiling fish
      stock or water
   15ml/1 tbsp tomato purée (paste)
   large pinch of saffron threads
   1 fresh bouquet garni, containing
      2 thyme sprigs, 2 bay leaves and
      2 fennel sprigs
   3kg/6½lb mixed fish, cleaned and
      cut into large chunks
   4 potatoes, peeled and thickly sliced
   salt, pepper and cayenne pepper
   a bowl of rouille (see Fish Soup) and
      a bowl of aioli (see Provençal Aioli
      with Salt Cod), to serve
For the garnish
   16 slices of French bread, toasted
      and rubbed with garlic
   30ml/2 tbsp chopped parsley

1 Heat the oil in a large pan. Add the onions, leeks, garlic and tomatoes. Cook until slightly softened. Stir in the stock or water, tomato purée and saffron. Add the bouquet garni and boil until the oil is amalgamated. Lower the heat; add the fish and potatoes.

COOK'S TIP
Suitable fish for Bouillabaisse include rascasse, conger eel, monkfish, red gurnard and John Dory.

2 Simmer the soup for 5–8 minutes, removing each type of fish as it becomes cooked. Continue to cook until the potatoes are very tender. Season well with salt, pepper and cayenne.

3 Divide the fish and potatoes among individual soup plates. Strain the soup and ladle it over the fish. Garnish with toasted French bread and parsley. Serve with rouille and aioli.

CLAM CHOWDER

If fresh clams are hard to find, use frozen or canned clams for this classic recipe from New England. Large clams should be cut into chunky pieces. Reserve a few clams in their shells for garnish, if you like. Traditionally, the soup is served with savoury saltine crackers. You should be able to find these in any good delicatessen.

SERVES FOUR

INGREDIENTS
    100g/3¾oz salt pork or thinly sliced
        unsmoked bacon, diced
    1 large onion, chopped
    2 potatoes, peeled and cut into
        1cm/½in cubes
    1 bay leaf
    1 fresh thyme sprig
    300ml/½ pint/1¼ cups milk
    400g/14oz cooked clams, cooking
        liquid reserved
    150ml/¼ pint/⅔ cup double
        (heavy) cream
    salt, ground white pepper and
        cayenne pepper
    finely chopped fresh parsley, to garnish

1 Put the salt pork or unsmoked bacon in a pan, and heat gently, stirring frequently, until the fat runs and the meat is starting to brown. Add the chopped onion and cook over a low heat until softened but not browned.

2 Add the cubed potatoes, the bay leaf and thyme sprig, stir well to coat with fat, then pour in the milk and reserved clam liquid and bring to the boil. Lower the heat and simmer for about 10 minutes, until the potatoes are tender but still firm. Lift out the bay leaf and thyme sprig and discard.

3 Remove the shells from most of the clams. Add all the clams to the pan and season to taste with salt, pepper and cayenne. Simmer gently for 5 minutes more, then stir in the cream. Heat until the soup is very hot, but do not let it boil. Pour into a tureen, garnish with the chopped parsley and serve.

CHINESE CRAB AND SWEETCORN SOUP

Frozen white crab meat works as well as fresh in this delicately flavoured soup.

SERVES FOUR

INGREDIENTS
    600ml/1 pint/2½ cups fish or
        chicken stock
    2.5cm/1in piece fresh root ginger,
        peeled and very finely sliced
    400g/14oz can creamed sweetcorn
    150g/5oz cooked white crab meat
    15ml/1 tbsp arrowroot or
        cornflour (cornstarch)
    15ml/1 tbsp rice wine or dry sherry
    15–30ml/1–2 tbsp light soy sauce
    1 egg white
    salt and ground white pepper
    shredded spring onions (scallions),
        to garnish

COOK'S TIP
This soup is sometimes made with whole kernel corn, but creamed corn gives a better texture. If you can't find it in a can, use thawed frozen creamed sweetcorn instead; the result will be just as good.

1 Put the stock and ginger in a large pan and bring to the boil. Stir in the creamed sweetcorn and bring back to the boil.

2 Switch off the heat and add the crab meat. Put the arrowroot or cornflour in a cup and stir in the rice wine or sherry to make a smooth paste; stir this into the soup. Cook over a low heat for about 3 minutes until the soup has thickened and is slightly glutinous in consistency. Add light soy sauce, salt and white pepper to taste.

3 In a bowl, whisk the egg white to a stiff foam. Gradually fold it into the soup. Ladle the soup into heated bowls, garnish each portion with spring onions and serve.

VARIATION
To make prawn (shrimp) and sweetcorn soup, substitute 150g/5oz/1¼ cups cooked peeled prawns for the crab meat. Chop the peeled prawns roughly and add to the soup at the beginning of step 2.

THAI FISH BROTH

LEMON GRASS, CHILLIES AND GALANGAL ARE AMONG THE FLAVOURINGS USED IN THIS FRAGRANT SOUP.

SERVES TWO TO THREE

INGREDIENTS

1 litre/1¾ pints/4 cups fish stock
4 lemon grass stalks
3 limes
2 small fresh hot red chillies, seeded and thinly sliced
2cm/¾in piece fresh galangal, peeled and thinly sliced
6 coriander (cilantro) stalks, with leaves
2 kaffir lime leaves, coarsely chopped (optional)
350g/12oz monkfish fillet, skinned and cut into 2.5cm/1in pieces
15ml/1 tbsp rice vinegar
45ml/3 tbsp Thai fish sauce (*nam pla*)
30ml/2 tbsp chopped coriander (cilantro) leaves, to garnish

1 Pour the stock into a pan and bring it to the boil. Meanwhile, slice the bulb end of the lemon grass stalks diagonally into pieces about 3mm/⅛in thick. Peel off four wide strips of lime rind with a vegetable peeler, taking care to avoid the white pith underneath which would make the soup bitter. Squeeze the limes and reserve the juice.

2 Add the sliced lemon grass, lime rind, chillies, galangal and coriander stalks to the stock, with the kaffir lime leaves, if using. Simmer for 1–2 minutes.

VARIATIONS
Prawns (shrimp), scallops, squid or sole can be substituted for the monkfish. If you use kaffir lime leaves, you will need the juice of only 2 limes.

3 Add the monkfish, rice vinegar and fish sauce, with half the reserved lime juice. Simmer for about 3 minutes, until the fish is just cooked. Lift out and discard the coriander stalks, taste the broth and add more lime juice if necessary; the soup should taste quite sour. Sprinkle with the coriander leaves and serve very hot.

MALAYSIAN PRAWN LAKSA

THIS SPICY PRAWN AND NOODLE SOUP TASTES JUST AS GOOD WHEN MADE WITH FRESH CRAB MEAT OR ANY FLAKED COOKED FISH. IF YOU ARE SHORT OF TIME OR CAN'T FIND ALL THE SPICY PASTE INGREDIENTS, BUY READY-MADE LAKSA PASTE, WHICH IS AVAILABLE FROM ASIAN STORES.

SERVES TWO TO THREE

INGREDIENTS

115g/4oz rice vermicelli or stir-fry
   rice noodles
15ml/1 tbsp vegetable or
   groundnut (peanut) oil
600ml/1 pint/2½ cups fish stock
400ml/14fl oz/1⅔ cups thin
   coconut milk
30ml/2 tbsp Thai fish sauce (*nam pla*)
½ lime
16–24 cooked peeled prawns (shrimp)
salt and cayenne pepper
60ml/4 tbsp chopped fresh coriander
   (cilantro) sprigs and leaves,
   to garnish
For the spicy paste
2 lemon grass stalks, finely chopped
2 fresh red chillies, seeded
   and chopped
2.5cm/1in piece fresh root ginger,
   peeled and sliced
2.5ml/½ tsp dried shrimp paste
2 garlic cloves, chopped
2.5ml/½ tsp ground turmeric
30ml/2 tbsp tamarind paste

1 Cook the rice vermicelli or noodles in a large pan of boiling salted water according to the instructions on the packet. Tip into a large strainer or colander, then rinse under cold water and drain. Keep warm.

2 To make the spicy paste, place all the prepared ingredients in a mortar and pound with a pestle. Alternatively, put the ingredients in a food processor and process until a smooth paste is formed.

3 Heat the vegetable or groundnut oil in a large pan, add the spicy paste and fry, stirring constantly, for a few moments to release all the flavours, but be careful not to let it burn.

4 Add the fish stock and coconut milk and bring to the boil. Stir in the fish sauce, then simmer for 5 minutes. Season with salt and cayenne , adding a squeeze of lime. Add the prawns and heat through for a few seconds.

5 Divide the noodles among two or three soup plates. Pour over the soup, making sure that each portion includes an equal number of prawns. Garnish with coriander and serve piping hot.

APPETIZERS

Fish and shellfish make the perfect light start to any meal, whatever the main course. Titillate your taste buds with refreshing Ceviche or that old favourite, Prawn Cocktail. Classic Oysters Rockefeller, and Gratin of Mussels with Pesto are as succulent as they are sophisticated, while deliciously crisp Devilled Whitebait provide piquancy and crunch. If you prefer fish to shellfish, Red Mullet Dolmades make an unusual appetizer.

CEVICHE

YOU CAN USE ALMOST ANY FIRM-FLESHED FISH FOR THIS SOUTH AMERICAN DISH, PROVIDED THAT IT IS PERFECTLY FRESH. THE FISH IS "COOKED" BY THE ACTION OF THE ACIDIC LIME JUICE. ADJUST THE AMOUNT OF CHILLI ACCORDING TO YOUR TASTE.

SERVES SIX

INGREDIENTS
   675g/1½lb halibut, turbot, sea bass
     or salmon fillets, skinned
   juice of 3 limes
   1–2 fresh red chillies, seeded and
     very finely chopped
   15ml/1 tbsp olive oil
   salt
For the garnish
   4 large firm tomatoes, peeled, seeded
     and diced
   1 ripe avocado, peeled, stoned
     (pitted) and diced
   15ml/1 tbsp lemon juice
   30ml/2 tbsp olive oil
   30ml/2 tbsp fresh coriander
     (cilantro) leaves

1 Cut the fish into strips measuring about 5 x 1cm/2 x ½in. Lay these in a shallow dish and pour over the lime juice, turning the strips to coat them all over in the juice. Cover with clear film (plastic wrap) and leave for 1 hour.

2 Combine all the garnish ingredients, except the coriander. Set aside.

3 Season the fish with salt and sprinkle over the chillies. Drizzle with the olive oil. Toss the fish in the mixture, then re-cover. Leave to marinate in the refrigerator for 15–30 minutes more.

4 To serve, divide the garnish among six plates. Spoon on the ceviche, sprinkle with coriander and serve.

MARINATED SMOKED HADDOCK FILLETS

THIS SIMPLE DISH COULD MAKE A LIGHT LUNCH, SERVED WITH A GREEN SALAD, AS WELL AS AN APPETIZER. EITHER WAY IT IS AN EXCELLENT SUMMER DISH AND CAN BE PREPARED IN ADVANCE.

SERVES SIX

INGREDIENTS
 450g/1lb undyed smoked haddock
  fillet, skinned
 1 onion, very thinly sliced
  into rings
 5–10ml/1–2 tsp Dijon mustard
 30ml/2 tbsp lemon juice
 90ml/6 tbsp olive oil
 45ml/3 tbsp dark rum
 12 small new potatoes, scrubbed
 30ml/2 tbsp chopped fresh dill, plus
  6 dill sprigs to garnish
 ground black pepper

COOK'S TIP

Try to get a large, thick haddock fillet. If all you can find are small pieces, you can still make the dish, but serve the pieces whole instead of slicing them.

1 Cut the fish fillet in half lengthways. Arrange the pieces in a single layer in a shallow non-metallic dish. Sprinkle the onion rings evenly over the top.

2 Whisk together the mustard, lemon juice and some pepper. Add the oil gradually, whisking. Pour two-thirds of the dressing over the fish. Cover the dish with clear film (plastic wrap) and leave the fish to marinate for 2 hours in a cool place. Sprinkle on the rum and leave for 1 hour more.

3 Cook the potatoes in boiling salted water until tender. Drain, cut in half and tip into a bowl. Cool until warm, then toss in the remaining dressing. Stir in the dill, cover and set aside.

4 Slice the haddock thinly, as for smoked salmon, or leave whole. Arrange on small plates and spoon over some marinade and onion rings. Pile the potato halves on one side of each plate and garnish each portion with dill. Serve chilled or at room temperature.

MOULES PROVENÇALES

EATING THESE DELECTABLE MUSSELS IS A MESSY AFFAIR, WHICH IS PART OF THEIR CHARM. HAND ROUND PLENTY OF CRUSTY FRENCH BREAD FOR MOPPING UP THE JUICES AND DON'T FORGET FINGERBOWLS OF WARM WATER AND A PLATE FOR DISCARDED SHELLS.

SERVES FOUR

INGREDIENTS

30ml/2 tbsp olive oil
200g/7oz rindless unsmoked streaky
  (fatty) bacon, cubed
1 onion, finely chopped
3 garlic cloves, finely chopped
1 bay leaf
15ml/1 tbsp chopped fresh mixed
  Provençal herbs, thyme, marjoram,
  basil, oregano and savory
15–30ml/1–2 tbsp sun-dried
  tomatoes in oil, chopped
4 large, very ripe tomatoes, peeled,
  seeded and chopped
50g/2oz/½ cup pitted black
  olives, chopped
105ml/7 tbsp dry white wine
2.25kg/5–5¼lb live mussels,
  scrubbed and bearded
salt and ground black pepper
60ml/4 tbsp coarsely chopped
  fresh parsley, to garnish

1 Heat the oil in a large pan. Fry the bacon until golden and crisp. Remove with a slotted spoon and set aside. Add the onion and garlic to the pan and cook gently until softened. Add the herbs, with both types of tomatoes. Cook gently for 5 minutes, stirring frequently. Stir in the olives and season.

2 Put the wine and mussels in another pan. Cover and shake over a high heat for 5 minutes until the mussels open. Discard any which remain closed.

3 Strain the cooking liquid into the pan containing the tomato sauce and boil until reduced by about one-third. Add the mussels and stir to coat them thoroughly with the sauce. Take out the bay leaf.

4 Divide the mussels and sauce among four heated dishes. Sprinkle over the fried bacon and chopped parsley and serve piping hot.

OYSTERS ROCKEFELLER

THIS IS THE PERFECT DISH FOR THOSE WHO PREFER THEIR OYSTERS LIGHTLY COOKED. AS A CHEAPER ALTERNATIVE, FOR THOSE WHO ARE NOT "SO RICH AS ROCKEFELLER", GIVE MUSSELS OR CLAMS THE SAME TREATMENT; THEY WILL ALSO TASTE DELICIOUS.

SERVES SIX

INGREDIENTS
  450g/1lb/3 cups coarse salt, plus
    extra to serve
  24 oysters, opened
  115g/4oz/½ cup butter
  2 shallots, finely chopped
  500g/1¼lb spinach leaves,
    finely chopped
  60ml/4 tbsp chopped fresh parsley
  60ml/4 tbsp chopped celery leaves
  90ml/6 tbsp fresh white breadcrumbs
  Tabasco sauce or cayenne pepper
  10–20ml/2–4 tsp Pernod or Ricard
  salt and ground black pepper
  lemon wedges, to serve

COOK'S TIP
If you prefer a smoother stuffing, process to a paste in a food processor or blender.

1 Preheat the oven to 220°C/425°F/ Gas 7. Make a bed of coarse salt on two large baking sheets. Set the oysters in the half-shell in the bed of salt to keep them steady. Set aside.

2 Melt the butter in a frying pan. Add the finely chopped shallots and cook them over a low heat for 2–3 minutes until they are softened. Stir in the spinach and let it wilt.

3 Add the parsley, celery leaves and breadcrumbs to the pan and cook gently for 5 minutes. Season with salt, pepper and Tabasco or cayenne.

4 Divide the stuffing among the oysters. Drizzle a few drops of Pernod or Ricard over each oyster, then bake for about 5 minutes, until bubbling and golden brown. Serve on a heated platter on a shallow salt bed with lemon wedges.

AROMATIC TIGER PRAWNS

THERE IS NO ELEGANT WAY TO EAT THESE AROMATIC PRAWNS — JUST HOLD THEM BY THE TAILS, PULL THEM OFF THE STICKS WITH YOUR FINGERS AND POP THEM INTO YOUR MOUTH.

SERVES FOUR

INGREDIENTS

16 raw tiger prawns (jumbo shrimp) or scampi (extra large shrimp) tails
2.5ml/½ tsp chilli powder
5ml/1 tsp fennel seeds
5 Sichuan or black peppercorns
1 star anise, broken into segments
1 cinnamon stick, broken into pieces
30ml/2 tbsp groundnut (peanut) or sunflower oil
2 garlic cloves, chopped
2cm/¾in piece fresh root ginger, peeled and finely chopped
1 shallot, chopped
30ml/2 tbsp water
30ml/2 tbsp rice vinegar
30ml/2 tbsp soft brown or palm sugar
salt and ground black pepper
lime slices and chopped spring onion (scallion), to garnish

1 Thread the prawns or scampi tails in pairs on eight wooden cocktail sticks. Set aside. Heat a frying pan, put in all the chilli powder, fennel seeds, Sichuan or black peppercorns, star anise and cinnamon stick and dry-fry for 1–2 minutes to release the flavours. Leave to cool, then grind the spices coarsely in a grinder or tip into a mortar and crush with a pestle.

2 Heat the groundnut or sunflower oil in a shallow pan, add the garlic, ginger and chopped shallot and then cook gently until very lightly coloured. Add the crushed spices and seasoning and cook the mixture gently for 2 minutes. Pour in the water and simmer, stirring, for 5 minutes.

3 Add the rice vinegar and soft brown or palm sugar, stir until dissolved, then add the prawns or scampi tails. Cook for 3–5 minutes, until the shellfish has turned pink, but is still very juicy. Serve hot, garnished with lime slices and spring onion.

COOK'S TIP
If you buy whole prawns (shrimp), remove the heads before cooking them.

PRAWN AND VEGETABLE CROSTINI

USE BOTTLED CARCIOFINI (TINY ARTICHOKE HEARTS PRESERVED IN OLIVE OIL) FOR THIS SIMPLE APPETIZER, WHICH CAN BE PREPARED VERY QUICKLY.

SERVES FOUR

INGREDIENTS

450g/1lb whole cooked prawns (shrimp), in the shell
4 thick slices of ciabatta bread, cut diagonally across
3 garlic cloves, peeled and 2 halved lengthways
60ml/4 tbsp olive oil
200g/7oz/2 cups small button (white) mushrooms, trimmed
12 drained bottled *carciofini*
60ml/4 tbsp chopped flat leaf parsley
salt and ground black pepper

COOK'S TIP
Don't be tempted to use thawed frozen prawns (shrimp), especially those that have been peeled; freshly cooked prawns in their shells are infinitely nicer.

1 Peel the prawns and remove the heads. Rub the ciabatta slices on both sides with the cut sides of the halved garlic cloves, drizzle with a little of the olive oil and toast in the oven or grill (broil) until lightly browned. Keep hot.

2 Finely chop the remaining garlic. Heat the remaining oil in a pan and gently cook the garlic until golden, but do not allow it to brown.

3 Add the mushrooms and stir to coat with oil. Season and sauté for about 2–3 minutes. Gently stir in the drained *carciofini*, then add the chopped flat leaf parsley.

4 Season again, then stir in the prawns and sauté briefly to warm through. Pile the prawn mixture on to the ciabatta, pour over any remaining cooking juices and serve immediately.

SCALLOPS WITH SAMPHIRE AND LIME

SAMPHIRE HAS A WONDERFUL TASTE AND AROMA OF THE SEA. IT IS THE PERFECT COMPLEMENT TO
SCALLOPS AND HELPS TO CREATE A VERY ATTRACTIVE STARTER.

SERVES FOUR

INGREDIENTS

225g/8oz fresh samphire
12 large or 24 queen scallops, out of
  the shell
300ml/½ pint/1¼ cups dry
  white wine
juice of 2 limes
15ml/1 tbsp groundnut (peanut) or
  vegetable oil
½ cucumber, peeled, seeded
  and diced
ground black pepper
chopped fresh parsley, to garnish

1 Wash the fresh samphire in several
changes of cold water. Drain, then trim
off any woody ends. Bring a pan of
water to the boil, then drop in the
samphire and cook for 3–5 minutes,
until tender but still crisp. Drain, refresh
under cold water and drain again.

2 If the scallops are large, cut them in
half horizontally. Detach the corals. In a
shallow pan, bring the wine to the boil
and cook until it is reduced by about
one-third. Lower the heat and add the
lime juice to the pan.

3 Add the scallops and corals and
poach gently for 3–4 minutes until the
scallops are just cooked, but still
opaque. Using a slotted spoon, lift out
the scallops and corals and set aside.

COOK'S TIP
Samphire grows wild in estuaries and
salt marshes in Europe and North
America. High-quality fishmongers
sometimes stock it.

4 Leave the cooking liquid to cool until
tepid, then whisk in the groundnut or
vegetable oil. Add the samphire,
cucumber, scallops and corals and toss
lightly to mix. Grind over some black
pepper, cover and leave at room
temperature for about 1 hour to allow
the flavours to develop. Divide the
mixture among four individual dishes and
then garnish with chopped fresh parsley.
Serve the dish at room temperature.

GRATIN OF MUSSELS WITH PESTO

THIS IS THE PERFECT APPETIZER FOR SERVING WHEN TIME IS SHORT, AS BOTH THE PESTO AND THE MUSSELS CAN BE PREPARED IN ADVANCE, AND THE DISH ASSEMBLED AND COOKED AT THE LAST MINUTE.

SERVES FOUR

INGREDIENTS
   36 large live mussels, scrubbed
      and bearded
   105ml/7 tbsp dry white wine
   60ml/4 tbsp finely chopped fresh
      flat leaf parsley
   1 garlic clove, finely chopped
   30ml/2 tbsp fresh white breadcrumbs
   60ml/4 tbsp olive oil
   chopped fresh basil, to garnish
   crusty bread, to serve
For the pesto
   2 fat garlic cloves, chopped
   2.5ml/½ tsp coarse salt
   100g/3¾oz/3 cups basil leaves
   25g/1oz/¼ cup pine nuts, chopped
   50g/2oz/⅔ cup freshly grated
      Parmesan cheese
   120ml/4fl oz/½ cup extra virgin
      olive oil

1 Put the mussels in a pan with the wine, clamp on the lid and shake over high heat for 3–4 minutes until the mussels have opened. Discard any which remain closed.

2 As soon as the mussels are cool enough to handle, strain the cooking liquid and keep it for another recipe. Discard the empty half-shells. Arrange the mussels in their half-shells in a single layer in four individual gratin dishes. Cover and set aside.

COOK'S TIP
Home-made pesto is best but when basil is out of season – or you are in a hurry – a jar may be used instead.

3 To make the pesto, put the chopped garlic and salt in a mortar and pound to a purée with a pestle. Then add the basil leaves and chopped pine nuts and crush to a thick paste. Work in the Parmesan cheese and, finally, gradually drip in enough olive oil to make a smooth and creamy paste. Alternatively, use a food processor.

4 Spoon pesto over the mussels placed in gratin dishes. Mix the parsley, garlic and breadcrumbs. Sprinkle over the mussels. Drizzle with the oil.

5 Preheat the grill (broiler) to high. Stand the dishes on a baking sheet and grill (broil) for 3 minutes. Garnish with basil and serve with crusty bread.

PRAWN COCKTAIL

THERE IS NO NICER APPETIZER THAN A GOOD, FRESH PRAWN COCKTAIL — AND NOTHING NASTIER THAN ONE IN WHICH SOGGY PRAWNS SWIM IN A THIN, VINEGARY SAUCE EMBEDDED IN LIMP LETTUCE. THIS RECIPE SHOWS JUST HOW GOOD A PRAWN COCKTAIL CAN BE.

SERVES SIX

INGREDIENTS
   60ml/4 tbsp double (heavy) cream,
     lightly whipped
   60ml/4 tbsp mayonnaise, preferably
     home-made
   60ml/4 tbsp tomato ketchup
   5–10ml/1–2 tsp Worcestershire sauce
   juice of 1 lemon
   ½ cos (romaine) lettuce or other very
     crisp lettuce
   450g/1lb/4 cups cooked peeled
     prawns (shrimp)
   salt, ground black pepper
     and paprika
   6 large whole cooked prawns (shrimp)
     in the shell, to garnish (optional)
   thinly sliced brown bread with butter
     and lemon wedges, to serve

1 Place the lightly whipped cream, mayonnaise and tomato ketchup in a small bowl and whisk lightly to combine. Add Worcestershire sauce to taste, then whisk in enough of the lemon juice to make a really tangy sauce.

COOK'S TIP
Partly peeled prawns (shrimp) make a pretty garnish. To prepare, carefully peel the body shell from the prawns and leave the tail "fan" for decoration.

2 Finely shred the lettuce and fill six individual glasses one-third full.

3 Stir the prawns into the sauce, then check the seasoning and spoon the prawn mixture generously over the lettuce. If you like, drape a whole cooked prawn over the edge of each glass and sprinkle each of the cocktails with ground black pepper and/or paprika. Serve immediately, with thinly sliced brown bread with butter and lemon wedges.

CRAB SALAD WITH ROCKET

IF THE DRESSED CRABS ARE REALLY SMALL, PILE THE SALAD BACK INTO THE SHELLS FOR AN ATTRACTIVE ALTERNATIVE PRESENTATION.

SERVES FOUR

INGREDIENTS
   4 small fresh dressed crabs
   1 small red (bell) pepper, seeded and
     finely chopped
   1 small red onion, finely chopped
   30ml/2 tbsp drained capers
   30ml/2 tbsp chopped fresh
     coriander (cilantro)
   grated rind and juice of 2 lemons
   Tabasco sauce
   salt and ground black pepper
   lemon rind strips, to garnish
For the rocket (arugula) salad
   40g/1½oz rocket (arugula) leaves
   30ml/2 tbsp sunflower oil
   15ml/1 tbsp fresh lime juice

1 Put the white and brown crab meat, red pepper, onion, capers and chopped coriander in a bowl. Add the lemon rind and juice and toss gently to mix together. Season with a few drops of Tabasco sauce, according to taste, and a little salt and pepper.

2 Wash the rocket leaves and pat dry on kitchen paper. Divide them among four plates. Mix together the oil and lime juice in a small bowl. Dress the rocket leaves, then pile the crab salad on top and serve garnished with lemon rind strips.

RED MULLET DOLMADES

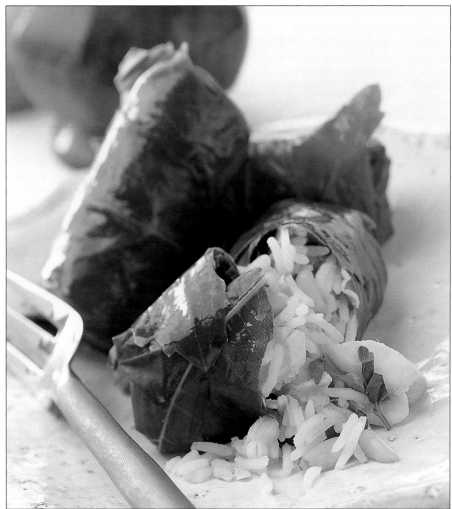

2 Remove the skin from the fish fillets and flake the flesh into a bowl. Gently stir in the cooked rice, pine nuts, the chopped parsley, and lemon rind and juice. Season the filling to taste with salt and ground black pepper.

3 Spoon 30–45ml/2–3 tbsp of the filling into the middle of each vine leaf. Roll up each filled leaf, tucking in the ends to make a secure package. Arrange the dolmades in an ovenproof dish, with the joins underneath. Then pour over the reserved cooking liquid and place the dolmades in the preheated oven for about 5 minutes, until they are thoroughly heated through.

4 Meanwhile, make the sauce. Mix the orange rind and juice and the shallots in a small pan and boil vigorously for a few minutes until the mixture is reduced and syrupy.

SERVES FOUR

INGREDIENTS
    225g/8oz red mullet or red snapper
      fillets, scaled
    45ml/3 tbsp dry white wine
    115g/4oz/1 cup cooked long
      grain rice
    25g/1oz/¼ cup pine nuts
    45ml/3 tbsp chopped fresh parsley
    grated rind and juice of ½ lemon
    8 vine leaves in brine, rinsed
      and dried
    salt and ground black pepper
For the orange butter sauce
    grated rind and juice of 2 oranges
    2 shallots, very finely chopped
    25g/1oz/2 tbsp chilled butter, diced

1 Preheat the oven to 200°C/400°F/ Gas 6. Put the fish fillets in a shallow pan and season with salt and pepper. Pour over the wine, bring to the boil, then lower the heat and poach the fish gently for about 3 minutes, until it is just cooked. Strain, reserving the cooking liquid.

5 Strain the sauce into a clean pan, discarding the shallots. Beat in the butter, one piece at a time. Reheat gently, but do not let the sauce boil. Drizzle the sauce over the hot dolmades and serve immediately.

SALMON AND SCALLOP BROCHETTES

WITH THEIR DELICATE COLOURS AND SUPERB FLAVOUR, THESE SKEWERS MAKE THE PERFECT OPENER FOR A SOPHISTICATED MEAL.

SERVES FOUR

INGREDIENTS

    8 lemon grass stalks
    225g/8oz salmon fillet, skinned
    8 queen scallops, with their corals
      if possible
    8 baby (pearl) onions, peeled
      and blanched
    ½ yellow (bell) pepper, cut into
      8 squares
    25g/1oz/2 tbsp butter
    juice of ½ lemon
    salt, ground white pepper
      and paprika
For the sauce
    30ml/2 tbsp dry vermouth
    50g/2oz/¼ cup butter
    5ml/1 tsp chopped fresh tarragon

1 Preheat the grill (broiler) to medium-high. Cut off the top 7.5–10cm/3–4in of each lemon grass stalk. Reserve the bulb ends for another dish. Cut the salmon fillet into twelve 2cm/¾in cubes. Thread the salmon, scallops, corals if available, onions and pepper squares on to the lemon grass and arrange the brochettes in a grill pan.

2 Melt the butter in a small pan, add the lemon juice and a pinch of paprika and then brush all over the brochettes. Grill (broil) the skewers for about 2–3 minutes on each side, turning and basting the brochettes every minute, until the fish and scallops are just cooked, but are still very juicy. Transfer to a platter and keep hot while you make the tarragon butter sauce.

3 Pour the dry vermouth and all the leftover cooking juices from the brochettes into a small pan and boil quite fiercely to reduce by half. Add the butter and melt, stirring constantly. Stir in the chopped fresh tarragon and add salt and ground white pepper to taste. Pour the tarragon butter sauce over the brochettes and serve.

SOFT-SHELL CRABS WITH CHILLI AND SALT

*IF FRESH SOFT-SHELL CRABS ARE UNAVAILABLE, YOU CAN BUY FROZEN ONES IN ASIAN SUPERMARKETS.
ALLOW TWO SMALL CRABS PER SERVING, OR ONE IF THEY ARE LARGE. ADJUST THE QUANTITY OF CHILLI
ACCORDING TO YOUR TASTE.*

SERVES FOUR

INGREDIENTS
    8 small soft-shell crabs, thawed
      if frozen
    50g/2oz/½ cup plain (all-purpose) flour
    60ml/4 tbsp groundnut (peanut) or
      vegetable oil
    2 large fresh red chillies, or 1 green
      and 1 red, seeded and thinly sliced
    4 spring onions (scallions) or a small
      bunch of garlic chives, chopped
    sea salt and ground black pepper
To serve
    shredded lettuce, mooli (daikon) and
      carrot
    light soy sauce

COOK'S TIP
The vegetables make a colourful bed for
the crabs. If you can't locate any mooli
(daikon), use celeriac instead.

1 Pat the crabs dry with kitchen paper.
Season the flour with pepper and coat
the crabs lightly with the mixture.

2 Heat the oil in a shallow pan until
very hot, then put in the crabs (you may
need to do this in two batches). Cook
for 2–3 minutes on each side, until the
crabs are golden brown but still juicy in
the middle. Drain the cooked crabs on
kitchen paper and keep hot.

3 Add the sliced chillies and spring
onions or garlic chives to the oil
remaining in the pan and cook gently
for about 2 minutes. Sprinkle over a
generous pinch of salt, then spread the
mixture on to the crabs.

4 Mix the shredded lettuce, mooli and
carrot together. Arrange on plates, top
each portion with two crabs and serve,
with light soy sauce for dipping.

DEVILLED WHITEBAIT

*SERVE THESE DELICIOUSLY CRISP LITTLE FISH WITH LEMON WEDGES AND THINLY SLICED BROWN BREAD
AND BUTTER, AND EAT THEM WITH YOUR FINGERS.*

SERVES FOUR

INGREDIENTS
    oil for deep-frying
    150ml/¼ pint/⅔ cup milk
    115g/4oz/1 cup plain (all-
      purpose) flour
    450g/1lb whitebait
    salt, ground black pepper and
      cayenne pepper

1 Heat the oil in a large pan or deep-
fryer. Put the milk in a shallow bowl and
the flour into a paper bag. Season it
with salt, pepper and a little cayenne.

COOK'S TIP
Most whitebait are sold frozen. Thaw
them before use and dry them thoroughly
on kitchen paper.

2 Dip a handful of the whitebait into the
bowl of milk, drain them well, then pop
them into the paper bag. Shake gently
to coat them evenly in the seasoned
flour. Repeat until all the fish have been
coated with flour. This is the easiest
method of flouring whitebait, but don't
add too many at once, or they will
stick together.

3 Heat the oil for deep-frying to 190°C/
375°F or until a small cube of stale
bread, dropped into the oil, browns in
20 seconds. Add a batch of whitebait,
preferably in a frying basket, and fry for
2–3 minutes, until crisp and golden
brown. Drain and keep hot while you fry
the rest. Sprinkle with more cayenne
and serve very hot.

MOUSSES, PÂTÉS AND TERRINES

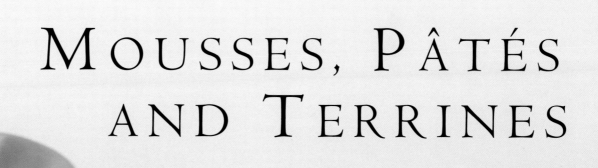

Soft-textured fish and shellfish can be puréed to produce attractive light-textured mousses, such as Smoked Fish and Asparagus Mousse. Hot Crab Soufflés make a substantial appetizer or light lunch or supper dish for a chilly day, and chunky Haddock and Smoked Salmon Terrine is ideal when the weather warms up. Celebrate summer with cold creamy Sea Trout Mousse. For the simplest of dishes, Smoked Mackerel Pâté takes only moments to prepare and is perennially popular.

SEA TROUT MOUSSE

This deliciously creamy mousse makes a little sea trout go a long way. It is equally good made with salmon if sea trout is unavailable.

SERVES SIX

INGREDIENTS
    250g/9oz sea trout fillet
    120ml/4fl oz/½ cup fish stock
    2 gelatine leaves, or 15ml/1 tbsp
        powdered gelatine
    juice of ½ lemon
    30ml/2 tbsp dry sherry or
        dry vermouth
    30ml/2 tbsp freshly grated Parmesan
    300ml/½ pint/1¼ cups
        whipping cream
    2 egg whites
    15ml/1 tbsp sunflower oil
    salt and ground white pepper
For the garnish
    5cm/2in piece of cucumber, with
        peel, thinly sliced and halved
    fresh dill or chervil

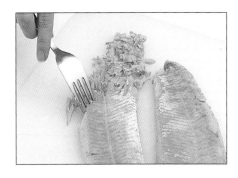

3 When the trout is cool enough to handle, remove the skin and flake the flesh. Pour the stock into a food processor or blender. Process briefly, then gradually add the flaked trout, lemon juice, sherry or vermouth and Parmesan through the feeder tube, continuing to process the mixture until it is smooth. Scrape into a large bowl and leave to cool completely.

4 Lightly whip the cream in a bowl; fold it into the cold trout mixture. Season to taste, then cover with clear film (plastic wrap) and chill until the mousse is just beginning to set. It should have the consistency of mayonnaise.

5 In a grease-free bowl, beat the egg whites with a pinch of salt until softly peaking. Using a large metal spoon, stir one-third into the trout mixture to slacken it, then fold in the rest.

6 Lightly grease six ramekins with the sunflower oil. Divide the mousse among the ramekins and level the surface. Place in the refrigerator for 2–3 hours, until set. Just before serving, arrange a few slices of cucumber and a small herb sprig on each mousse and add a little chopped dill or chervil.

1 Put the sea trout in a shallow pan. Pour in the fish stock and heat to simmering point. Poach the fish for about 3–4 minutes, until it is lightly cooked. Strain the stock into a jug (pitcher) and leave the trout to cool.

2 Add the gelatine to the hot stock and stir until it has dissolved completely. Set aside until required.

COOK'S TIP
Serve the mousse with Melba toast, if you like. Toast thin slices of bread on both sides under the grill (broiler), then cut off the crusts and slice each piece of toast in half horizontally. Return to the grill pan, untoasted sides up, and grill (broil) again. The thin slices will swiftly brown and curl, so watch them closely.

QUENELLES OF SOLE

TRADITIONALLY, THESE LIGHT FISH "DUMPLINGS" ARE MADE WITH PIKE, BUT THEY ARE EVEN BETTER MADE WITH SOLE OR OTHER WHITE FISH. IF YOU ARE FEELING EXTRAVAGANT, SERVE THEM WITH A CREAMY SHELLFISH SAUCE STUDDED WITH CRAYFISH TAILS OR PRAWNS.

SERVES SIX

INGREDIENTS

450g/1lb sole fillets, skinned and cut into large pieces
4 egg whites
600ml/1 pint/2½ cups double (heavy) cream
salt, ground white pepper and grated nutmeg

For the sauce

1 small shallot, finely chopped
60ml/4 tbsp dry vermouth
120ml/4fl oz/½ cup fish stock
150ml/¼ pint/⅔ cup double (heavy) cream
50g/2oz/¼ cup cold butter, diced
chopped fresh parsley, to garnish

1 Check the sole for stray bones, then put the pieces in a blender or food processor. Add a generous pinch of salt and a grinding of pepper. Switch on and, with the motor running, add the egg whites one at a time through the feeder tube to make a smooth purée. Press the purée through a metal sieve placed over a bowl. Stand the bowl of purée in a larger bowl and surround it with plenty of crushed ice or ice cubes.

2 Whip the cream until very thick and floppy, but not stiff. Gradually fold it into the fish mousse, making sure each spoonful has been absorbed completely before adding the next. Season with salt and pepper, then stir in nutmeg to taste. Cover the bowl of mousse and transfer it, still in its bowl of ice, to the refrigerator. Chill for several hours.

3 To make the sauce, combine the shallot, vermouth and fish stock in a small pan. Bring to the boil and cook until reduced by half. Add the cream and boil again until the sauce has the consistency of single (light) cream. Strain, return to the pan and whisk in the butter, one piece at a time, until the sauce is very creamy. Season and keep hot, but do not let it boil.

4 Bring a wide shallow pan of lightly salted water to the boil, then reduce the heat so that the water surface barely trembles. Using two tablespoons dipped in hot water, shape the fish mousse into ovals. As each quenelle is shaped, slip it into the simmering water.

5 Poach the quenelles in batches for 8–10 minutes, until they feel just firm to the touch, but are still slightly creamy inside. As each is cooked, lift it out on a slotted spoon, drain on kitchen paper and keep hot. When all the quenelles are cooked, arrange them on heated plates. Pour the sauce around. Serve garnished with parsley.

COOK'S TIP
Keep the heat low when poaching; quenelles disintegrate in boiling water.

SMOKED MACKEREL PÂTÉ

SOME OF THE MOST DELICIOUS DISHES ARE ALSO THE SIMPLEST TO MAKE. SERVE THIS POPULAR PÂTÉ WITH WARMED MELBA TOAST AS AN APPETIZER, OR FOR A LIGHT LUNCH WITH WHOLEMEAL TOAST.

SERVES SIX

INGREDIENTS
  4 smoked mackerel fillets, skinned
  225g/8oz/1 cup cream cheese
  1–2 garlic cloves, finely chopped
  juice of 1 lemon
  30ml/2 tbsp chopped fresh chervil,
    parsley or chives
  15ml/1 tbsp Worcestershire sauce
  salt and cayenne pepper
  fresh chives, to garnish
  warmed Melba toast, to serve

VARIATION
Use peppered mackerel fillets for a more piquant flavour. This pâté can be made with smoked haddock or kipper (smoked herring) fillets.

1 Break up the mackerel and put it in a food processor. Add the cream cheese, garlic, lemon juice and herbs.

2 Process the mixture until it is fairly smooth but still has a slightly chunky texture, then add Worcestershire sauce, salt and cayenne pepper to taste. Process to mix, then spoon the pâté into a dish, cover with clear film (plastic wrap) and chill. Garnish with chives and serve with Melba toast.

BRANDADE OF SALT COD

THERE ARE ALMOST AS MANY VERSIONS OF THIS CREAMY SALT COD PURÉE AS THERE ARE REGIONS OF FRANCE. SOME CONTAIN MASHED POTATOES, OTHERS TRUFFLES. THIS COMPARATIVELY LIGHT RECIPE INCLUDES GARLIC, BUT YOU CAN OMIT IT AND SERVE THE BRANDADE ON TOASTED SLICES OF FRENCH BREAD RUBBED WITH GARLIC IF YOU LIKE.

SERVES SIX

INGREDIENTS
  200g/7oz salt cod
  250ml/8fl oz/1 cup extra virgin
    olive oil
  4 garlic cloves, crushed
  250ml/8fl oz/1 cup double (heavy) or
    whipping cream
  freshly ground white pepper
  shredded spring onions (scallions),
    to garnish
  herbed crispbread, to serve

COOK'S TIP
You can purée the fish mixture in a mortar with a pestle. This gives a better texture, but is notoriously hard work.

1 Soak the fish in cold water for 24 hours, changing the water often. Drain. Cut into pieces, place in a shallow pan and pour in cold water to cover. Heat the water until simmering, then poach the fish for 8 minutes, until just cooked. Drain, then remove the skin and bones.

2 Combine the olive oil and garlic in a small pan and heat to just below boiling point. In another pan, heat the cream until it starts to simmer.

3 Put the cod into a food processor, process it briefly, then gradually add alternate amounts of the garlic-flavoured olive oil and cream, while continuing to process the mixture. The aim is to create a purée with the consistency of mashed potatoes.

4 Add pepper to taste, then scoop the brandade into a serving bowl. Garnish with shredded spring onions and serve warm with herbed crispbread.

HOT CRAB SOUFFLÉS

THESE DELICIOUS LITTLE SOUFFLÉS MUST BE SERVED AS SOON AS THEY ARE READY, SO SEAT YOUR GUESTS AT THE TABLE BEFORE TAKING THE SOUFFLÉS OUT OF THE OVEN.

SERVES SIX

INGREDIENTS
    50g/2oz/¼ cup butter
    45ml/3 tbsp fine wholemeal (whole-
        wheat) breadcrumbs
    4 spring onions (scallions),
        finely chopped
    15ml/1 tbsp Malaysian or mild
        Madras curry powder
    25g/1oz/2 tbsp plain (all-
        purpose) flour
    105ml/7 tbsp coconut milk or milk
    150ml/¼ pint/⅔ cup
        whipping cream
    4 egg yolks
    225g/8oz white crab meat
    mild green Tabasco sauce
    6 egg whites
    salt and ground black pepper

1 Use some of the butter to grease six ramekins or a 1.75 litre/3 pint/7 cup soufflé dish. Sprinkle in the fine wholemeal breadcrumbs, roll the dishes or dish around to coat the base and sides completely, then tip out the excess breadcrumbs. Preheat the oven to 200°C/400°F/Gas 6.

2 Melt the remaining butter in a pan, add the spring onions and Malaysian or mild Madras curry powder and cook over a low heat for about 1 minute, until softened. Stir in the flour and cook for 1 minute more.

3 Gradually add the coconut milk or milk and cream, stirring constantly. Cook until smooth and thick. Remove the pan from the heat, stir in the egg yolks, then the crab. Season with salt, black pepper and Tabasco sauce.

4 In a grease-free bowl, beat the egg whites stiffly with a pinch of salt. Using a metal spoon, stir one-third into the mixture to slacken it; fold in the rest. Spoon into the dishes or dish.

5 Bake until well-risen and golden brown, and just firm to the touch. Individual soufflés will be ready in about 8 minutes; a large soufflé will take 15–20 minutes. Serve immediately.

SMOKED FISH <u>AND</u> ASPARAGUS MOUSSE

THIS ELEGANT MOUSSE LOOKS VERY SPECIAL WITH ITS STUDDING OF ASPARAGUS AND SMOKED SALMON. SERVE A MUSTARD AND DILL DRESSING SEPARATELY IF YOU LIKE.

SERVES EIGHT

INGREDIENTS

15ml/1 tbsp powdered gelatine
juice of 1 lemon
105ml/7 tbsp fish stock
50g/2oz/¼ cup butter, plus extra
   for greasing
2 shallots, finely chopped
225g/8oz smoked trout fillets
105ml/7 tbsp sour cream
225g/8oz/1 cup low-fat cream cheese
   or cottage cheese
1 egg white
12 spinach leaves, blanched
12 fresh asparagus spears,
   lightly cooked
115g/4oz smoked salmon, cut into
   long strips
salt
shredded beetroot (beet) and leaves,
   to garnish

4 Grease a 1 litre/1¾ pint/4 cup loaf tin (pan) or terrine with butter, then line it with the spinach leaves. Carefully spread half the trout mousse over the spinach-covered base, arrange the asparagus spears on top, then cover with the remaining trout mousse.

5 Arrange the smoked salmon strips lengthways on the mousse and fold over the overhanging spinach leaves. Cover with clear film (plastic wrap) and chill for 4 hours, until set. To serve, remove the clear film, turn out on to a serving dish and garnish.

1 Sprinkle the gelatine over the lemon juice and leave until spongy. In a small pan, heat the fish stock, then add the soaked gelatine and stir to dissolve completely. Set aside. Melt the butter in a small pan, add the shallots and cook gently until softened but not coloured.

2 Break up the smoked trout fillets and put them in a food processor with the shallots, sour cream, stock mixture and cream or cottage cheese. Process until smooth, then spoon into a bowl.

3 In a clean bowl, beat the egg white with a pinch of salt to soft peaks. Fold into the fish. Cover the bowl; chill for 30 minutes or until starting to set.

STRIPED FISH TERRINE

SERVE THIS ATTRACTIVE TERRINE COLD OR JUST WARM, WITH A HOLLANDAISE SAUCE IF YOU LIKE.
IT IS IDEAL AS AN APPETIZER OR LIGHT LUNCH DISH.

SERVES EIGHT

INGREDIENTS
    15ml/1 tbsp sunflower oil
    450g/1lb salmon fillet, skinned
    450g/1lb sole fillets, skinned
    3 egg whites
    105ml/7 tbsp double (heavy) cream
    15ml/1 tbsp fresh chives,
      finely chopped
    juice of 1 lemon
    115g/4oz/1 cup fresh or frozen
      peas, cooked
    5ml/1 tsp chopped fresh mint leaves
    salt, ground white pepper and
      grated nutmeg
    thinly sliced cucumber, salad cress
      and chives, to garnish

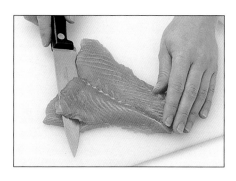

1 Grease a 1 litre/1¾ pint/4 cup loaf tin (pan) or terrine with the oil. Slice the salmon thinly; cut it and the sole into long strips, 2.5cm/1in wide. Preheat the oven to 200°C/400°F/Gas 6.

2 Line the terrine neatly with alternate slices of salmon and sole, leaving the ends overhanging the edge. You should be left with about a third of the salmon and half the sole.

3 In a grease-free bowl, beat the egg whites with a pinch of salt until they form soft peaks. Purée the remaining sole in a food processor. Spoon into a mixing bowl, season, then fold in two-thirds of the egg whites, followed by two-thirds of the cream. Put half the mixture into a second bowl; stir in the chives. Add nutmeg to the first bowl.

4 Purée the remaining salmon, scrape it into a bowl; add the lemon juice. Fold in the remaining whites, then cream.

5 Purée the peas with the mint. Season the mixture and spread it over the base of the terrine, smoothing the surface with a spatula. Spoon over the sole with chives mixture and spread evenly.

6 Add the salmon mixture, then finish with the plain sole mixture. Cover with the overhanging fish fillets and make a lid of oiled foil. Stand the terrine in a roasting pan and pour in enough boiling water to come halfway up the sides.

7 Bake for 15–20 minutes, until the top fillets are just cooked and the mousse feels springy. Remove the foil, lay a wire rack over the top of the terrine and invert both rack and terrine on to a lipped baking sheet to catch the cooking juices that drain out. Keep these to make fish stock or soup.

8 Leaving the tin in place, let the terrine stand for about 15 minutes, then turn the terrine over again. Invert it on to a serving dish and lift off the tin carefully. Serve warm, or chill in the refrigerator first and serve cold. Garnish with thinly sliced cucumber, salad cress and chives before serving.

COOK'S TIPS
• Pop the salmon into the freezer about 1 hour before slicing it. If it is almost frozen, it will be much easier to slice.
• You can line the tin (pan) or terrine with oven-safe clear film (plastic wrap) after greasing and before adding the salmon and sole strips. This makes it easier to turn out the terrine.

HADDOCK AND SMOKED SALMON TERRINE

THIS SUBSTANTIAL TERRINE MAKES A SUPERB DISH FOR A SUMMER BUFFET, ACCOMPANIED BY DILL MAYONNAISE OR A FRESH MANGO SALSA.

SERVES TEN TO TWELVE AS AN APPETIZER, SIX TO EIGHT AS A MAIN COURSE

INGREDIENTS

15ml/1 tbsp sunflower oil,
  for greasing
350g/12oz oak-smoked salmon
900g/2lb haddock fillets, skinned
2 eggs, lightly beaten
105ml/7 tbsp crème fraîche
30ml/2 tbsp drained capers
30ml/2 tbsp drained soft green or
  pink peppercorns
salt and ground white pepper
crème fraîche, peppercorns and fresh
  dill and rocket (arugula), to garnish

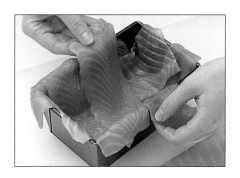

1 Preheat the oven to 200°C/400°F/ Gas 6. Grease a 1 litre/1¾ pint/4 cup loaf tin (pan) or terrine with the oil. Use some of the salmon to line the tin or terrine; let some of the ends overhang the mould. Reserve the remaining smoked salmon until needed.

2 Cut two long slices of haddock the length of the tin or terrine and set aside. Cut the rest of the haddock into small pieces. Season all the haddock with salt and pepper.

3 Combine the eggs, crème fraîche, capers and green or pink peppercorns in a bowl. Season with salt and pepper; stir in the small pieces of haddock. Spoon the mixture into the mould until it is one-third full. Smooth the surface with a spatula.

4 Wrap the long haddock fillets in the reserved smoked salmon. Lay them on top of the layer of the fish mixture in the tin or terrine.

5 Fill the tin or terrine with the rest of the fish mixture, smooth the surface and fold the overhanging pieces of smoked salmon over the top. Cover tightly with a double thickness of foil. Tap the terrine to settle the contents.

6 Stand the terrine in a roasting pan and pour in boiling water to come halfway up the sides. Place in the oven and cook for 45 minutes–1 hour, until the filling is just set.

7 Take the terrine out of the roasting pan, but do not remove the foil cover. Place two or three large heavy cans on the foil to weight it and leave until cold. Chill in the refrigerator for 24 hours.

8 About an hour before serving, remove the terrine from the refrigerator, lift off the weights and remove the foil. Carefully invert the terrine on to a serving plate and lift off the loaf tin or terrine.

9 Cut the terrine into thick slices using a sharp knife and serve, garnished with crème fraîche, peppercorns and fronds of dill and rocket leaves.

VARIATION
Use any thick white fish fillets for this terrine: try halibut or Arctic bass.

SMOKED HADDOCK AND AVOCADO MOUSSE

THE FRESH-TASTING SALSA COMPLEMENTS THE SMOOTH CREAMINESS OF THE MOUSSE.

SERVES SIX

INGREDIENTS

225g/8oz undyed smoked haddock
   fillets, skinned
½ onion, cut into thick rings
25g/1oz/2 tbsp butter
1 bay leaf
150ml/¼ pint/⅔ cup milk
1 ripe avocado
2 gelatine leaves, or 15ml/1 tbsp
   powdered gelatine
30ml/2 tbsp dry white wine
105ml/7 tbsp double (heavy) cream
1 egg white
salt, ground white pepper and
   grated nutmeg
For the salsa
3 tomatoes, peeled, seeded
   and diced
1 avocado
1 small red onion, finely chopped
1–2 garlic cloves, finely chopped
1 large fresh green chilli, seeded and
   finely chopped
45ml/3 tbsp extra virgin olive oil
juice of 1 lime
12 lime slices, to garnish

1 Arrange the fish in a single layer in a large shallow pan and lay the onion rings on top. Dot with butter, season with pepper, add the bay leaf and pour over the milk. Poach gently over a low heat for 5 minutes, or until the fish flakes easily when tested with the tip of a sharp knife. Remove the fish using a slotted spoon and leave to cool.

VARIATION
Undyed smoked cod can be used instead of the smoked haddock.

2 Using a slotted spoon, lift out and discard the bay leaf and onion. Set the pan over a high heat and boil the milk until it has reduced by about two-thirds. Flake the fish into a food processor and strain over the reduced milk. Process until smooth.

3 Spoon the fish mixture into a bowl. Peel the avocado and cut the flesh into 5mm/¼in dice. Fold into the fish purée.

4 In a small pan, soak the gelatine leaves in a little cold water until softened. If using powdered gelatine, sprinkle it over 30ml/2 tbsp cold water and leave until spongy. Add the wine to the softened gelatine and heat gently until completely dissolved, stirring constantly. Pour on to the fish mixture and mix well.

5 Lightly whip the cream in a bowl. In a second, grease-free bowl, beat the egg white with a pinch of salt until stiff. Fold the cream, then the egg white into the fish mixture. Season with salt and pepper and add a little nutmeg.

6 Pour the mixture into six ramekins or moulds, cover with clear film (plastic wrap) and chill for about 1 hour.

7 Meanwhile, make the salsa. Put the diced tomatoes in a bowl. Peel and dice the avocado and add it to the tomatoes with the onion, garlic and chilli. Add the olive oil and lime juice, with salt and pepper to taste. Chill until needed.

8 To release the mousse, dip the moulds into hot water for a couple of seconds, invert on to individual plates and give each mould a sharp tap. Put a spoonful of salsa on each plate and a little on the top of each mousse. Make a cut to the centre of each slice of lime and twist a couple of slices on to each plate. Serve with the remaining salsa.

SALADS

What could be nicer on a warm day than a refreshing fish or shellfish salad? Take a fresh look at fish as a salad ingredient. Meaty tuna, swordfish, skate and hake make ideal main-course medleys, while lighter offerings such as Insalata di Mare and Asparagus and Langoustine Salad are perfect for summertime al fresco lunches. If you're looking for something out of the ordinary, Warm Monkfish Salad with pine nuts makes an unusual and delicious dish, and Red Mullet with Raspberry Dressing is an unexpected delight.

FRESH TUNA SALAD NIÇOISE

FRESH TUNA TRANSFORMS THIS CLASSIC COLOURFUL SALAD FROM THE SOUTH OF FRANCE INTO SOMETHING REALLY SPECIAL.

SERVES FOUR

INGREDIENTS
- 4 tuna steaks, about 150g/5oz each
- 30ml/2 tbsp olive oil
- 225g/8oz fine green beans, trimmed
- 1 small cos (romaine) lettuce or
   2 Little Gem (Bibb) lettuces
- 4 new potatoes, boiled
- 4 ripe tomatoes, or
   12 cherry tomatoes
- 2 red (bell) peppers, seeded and cut
   into thin strips
- 4 hard-boiled (hard-cooked) eggs
- 8 drained anchovy fillets in oil,
   halved lengthways
- 16 large black olives
- salt and ground black pepper
- 12 fresh basil leaves, to garnish

For the dressing
- 15ml/1 tbsp red wine vinegar
- 90ml/6 tbsp olive oil
- 1 fat garlic clove, crushed

1 Brush the tuna on both sides with a little olive oil and season with salt and pepper. Heat a ridged griddle pan or the grill (broiler) until very hot, then cook the tuna steaks for 1–2 minutes on each side; the flesh should still be pink and juicy in the middle. Set aside.

2 Cook the beans in a pan of lightly salted boiling water for 4–5 minutes or until crisp-tender. Drain, refresh under cold water and drain again.

3 Separate the lettuce leaves and wash and dry them. Arrange them on four individual serving plates. Slice the potatoes and tomatoes, if large (leave cherry tomatoes whole) and divide them among the plates. Arrange the fine green beans and red pepper strips over them.

4 Shell the hard-boiled eggs, cut them into thick slices. Place two half eggs on each plate with an anchovy fillet draped over. Sprinkle four olives on to each plate.

5 To make the dressing, whisk together the vinegar, olive oil and garlic and seasoning to taste. Drizzle over the salads, arrange the tuna steaks on top, sprinkle over the basil and serve.

COOK'S TIP
To intensify the flavour of the (bell) peppers and improve their texture, grill (broil) them until the skins are charred, then put them in a bowl and cover with several layers of kitchen paper. Leave for 10–15 minutes, then rub off the skins.

INSALATA DI MARE

YOU CAN VARY THE FISH IN THIS ITALIAN SALAD ACCORDING TO WHAT IS AVAILABLE, BUT TRY TO INCLUDE AT LEAST TWO KINDS OF SHELLFISH AND SOME SQUID. THE SALAD IS GOOD WARM OR COLD.

SERVES SIX AS AN APPETIZER,
FOUR AS A MAIN COURSE

INGREDIENTS
    450g/1lb live mussels, scrubbed
        and bearded
    450g/1lb small clams, scrubbed
    105ml/7 tbsp dry white wine
    225g/8oz squid, cleaned
    4 large scallops, with their corals
    30ml/2 tbsp olive oil
    2 garlic cloves, finely chopped
    1 small dried red chilli, crumbled
    225g/8oz whole cooked prawns
        (shrimp), in the shell
    6–8 large chicory (Belgian
        endive) leaves
    6–8 radicchio leaves
    15ml/1 tbsp chopped flat leaf
        parsley, to garnish
For the dressing
    5ml/1 tsp Dijon mustard
    30ml/2 tbsp white wine vinegar
    5ml/1 tsp lemon juice
    120ml/4fl oz/½ cup extra virgin
        olive oil
    salt and ground black pepper

1 Put the mussels and clams in a large pan with the white wine. Cover and cook over a high heat, shaking the pan occasionally, for about 4 minutes, until they have opened. Discard any that remain closed. Use a slotted spoon to transfer the shellfish to a bowl, then strain and reserve the cooking liquid and set it aside.

2 Cut the squid into thin rings; chop the tentacles. Leave small squid whole. Halve the scallops horizontally.

3 Heat the oil in a frying pan, add the garlic, chilli, squid, scallops and corals, and sauté for about 2 minutes, until just cooked and tender. Lift the squid and scallops out of the pan; reserve the oil.

4 When the shellfish are cool enough to handle, shell them, keeping a dozen of each in the shell. Peel all but 6–8 of the prawns. Pour the shellfish cooking liquid into a small pan, set over a high heat and reduce by half. Mix all the shelled and unshelled mussels and clams with the squid and scallops, then add the prawns.

5 To make the dressing, whisk the mustard with the vinegar and lemon juice and season to taste. Add the olive oil, whisk vigorously, then whisk in the reserved cooking liquid and the oil from the frying pan. Pour the dressing over the shellfish mixture and toss lightly to coat well.

6 Arrange the chicory and radicchio leaves around the edge of a large serving dish and pile the mixed shellfish salad into the centre. Sprinkle with the chopped flat leaf parsley and serve immediately or chill first.

QUEEN SCALLOP <u>AND</u> GREEN BEAN SALAD

IF YOU LIKE, USE LIGHTLY COOKED MANGETOUTS INSTEAD OF THE FINE GREEN BEANS.

SERVES FOUR

INGREDIENTS

  115g/4oz fine green beans, trimmed
  2 good handfuls of frisée or Batavia
    lettuce leaves, finely shredded
  15g/½oz/1 tbsp butter
  15ml/1 tbsp hazelnut oil
  20 shelled queen scallops, with
    corals if possible
  2 spring onions (scallions), very
    thinly sliced
  salt and ground black pepper
  4 fresh chervil sprigs, to garnish
For the dressing
  10ml/2 tsp sherry vinegar
  30ml/2 tbsp hazelnut oil
  15ml/1 tbsp finely chopped fresh
    mint leaves

1 Cook the beans in a pan of lightly salted boiling water for about 5 minutes, until crisp-tender. Drain, refresh under cold water, drain again and set aside.

2 Wash and dry the salad leaves; put in a bowl. Mix the dressing, season, pour over the salad and toss. Divide the salad among four serving plates.

3 Heat the butter and hazelnut oil in a frying pan until sizzling, then add the scallops and their corals and sauté for about 1 minute, tossing the scallops in the fat until they have just turned opaque. Stir in the green beans and spring onions. Spoon the vegetables over the salad and pile the scallops and corals into a tower. Garnish and serve.

RED MULLET <u>WITH</u> RASPBERRY DRESSING

THE COMBINATION OF RED MULLET AND RASPBERRY VINEGAR IS DELICIOUS IN THIS FIRST-COURSE SALAD. KEEP TO THE "RED" THEME BY INCLUDING SALAD LEAVES SUCH AS RED OAKLEAF LETTUCE AND BABY RED-STEMMED CHARD. IF RED MULLET IS NOT AVAILABLE, USE SMALL RED SNAPPER FILLETS.

SERVES FOUR

INGREDIENTS

  8 red mullet or red snapper
    fillets, scaled
  15ml/1 tbsp olive oil
  15ml/1 tbsp raspberry vinegar
  175g/6oz mixed dark green and red
    salad leaves, such as lamb's lettuce
    (corn salad), radicchio, oakleaf
    lettuce and rocket (arugula)
  salt and ground black pepper
For the raspberry dressing
  115g/4oz/1 cup raspberries, puréed
    and sieved
  30ml/2 tbsp raspberry vinegar
  60ml/4 tbsp extra virgin olive oil
  2.5ml/½ tsp caster (superfine) sugar

COOK'S TIP
To make the raspberry purée, process the fruit in a blender or food processor, then press it through a strainer.

1 Lay the fish fillets in a shallow dish. Whisk together the olive oil and raspberry vinegar, add a pinch of salt and drizzle the mixture over the fish. Cover and leave to marinate for 1 hour.

2 Meanwhile, whisk together the dressing ingredients and season to taste.

3 Wash and dry the salad leaves, put them in a bowl, pour over most of the dressing and toss lightly.

4 Heat a ridged griddle pan or frying pan until very hot, put in the fish fillets and cook for 2–3 minutes on each side, until just tender. Cut the fillets diagonally in half to make rough diamond shapes.

5 Arrange a tall heap of salad in the middle of each serving plate. Prop up four fish fillet halves on the salad on each plate with the reserved dressing spooned around. Serve.

Piquant Prawn Salad

The Thai-inspired dressing adds a superb flavour to the noodles and prawns. This delicious salad can be served warm or cold, and will serve six as an appetizer.

SERVES FOUR

INGREDIENTS

   200g/7oz rice vermicelli
   8 baby corn cobs, halved
   150g/5oz mangetouts (snow peas)
   15ml/1 tbsp stir-fry oil
   2 garlic cloves, finely chopped
   2.5cm/1in piece fresh root ginger,
     peeled and finely chopped
   1 fresh red or green chilli, seeded
     and finely chopped
   450g/1lb raw peeled tiger prawns
     (jumbo shrimp)
   4 spring onions (scallions), thinly sliced
   15ml/1 tbsp sesame seeds, toasted
   1 lemon grass stalk, thinly shredded,
     to garnish
For the dressing
   15ml/1 tbsp chopped chives
   15ml/1 tbsp Thai fish sauce (*nam pla*)
   5ml/1 tsp soy sauce
   45ml/3 tbsp groundnut (peanut) oil
   5ml/1 tsp sesame oil
   30ml/2 tbsp rice vinegar

1 Put the rice vermicelli in a wide heatproof bowl, pour over boiling water and leave for 5 minutes. Drain, refresh under cold water and drain well again. Tip back into the bowl and set aside until required.

2 Boil or steam the corn cobs and mangetouts for about 3 minutes; they should still be crunchy. Refresh under cold water and drain. Now make the dressing. Mix all the ingredients in a screw-top jar, close tightly and shake well to combine.

3 Heat the oil in a large frying pan or wok. Add the garlic, ginger and red or green chilli and cook for 1 minute. Add the tiger prawns and stir-fry for about 3 minutes, until they have just turned pink. Stir in the spring onions, corn cobs, mangetouts and sesame seeds, and toss lightly to mix.

4 Tip the contents of the pan or wok over the rice vermicelli or noodles. Pour the dressing on top and toss well. Serve, garnished with lemon grass, or chill for an hour before serving.

HAKE AND POTATO SALAD

HAKE IS A "MEATY" FISH THAT IS EXCELLENT SERVED COLD IN A SALAD. HERE THE FLAVOUR IS ENHANCED WITH A PIQUANT DRESSING.

SERVES FOUR

INGREDIENTS
  450g/1lb hake fillets
  150ml/¼ pint/⅔ cup fish stock
  1 onion, thinly sliced
  1 bay leaf
  450g/1lb cooked baby new potatoes, halved unless tiny
  1 red (bell) pepper, seeded and diced
  115g/4oz/1 cup petits pois (baby peas), cooked
  2 spring onions (scallions), sliced
  ½ cucumber, unpeeled and diced
  4 large red lettuce leaves
  salt and ground black pepper
For the dressing
  150ml/¼ pint/⅔ cup Greek (US strained plain) yogurt
  30ml/2 tbsp olive oil
  juice of ½ lemon
  15–30ml/1–2 tbsp capers
To garnish
  2 hard-boiled (hard-cooked) eggs, finely chopped
  15ml/1 tbsp chopped fresh parsley
  15ml/1 tbsp finely chopped chives

1 Put the hake fillets in a large, shallow pan with the fish stock, onion slices and bay leaf. Bring to the boil over a medium heat, then lower the heat and poach the fish gently for about 10 minutes until it flakes easily when tested with the tip of a sharp knife. Leave it to cool, then remove the skin and any bones, and separate the flesh into large flakes.

2 Put the baby new potatoes in a bowl with the red pepper, petits pois, spring onions and cucumber. Gently stir in the flaked hake and season with salt and pepper.

3 Make the dressing by stirring all the ingredients together in a bowl or jug (pitcher). Season and spoon or pour over the salad. Toss gently.

4 Place a lettuce leaf on each plate and spoon the salad over it. Mix the finely chopped hard-boiled eggs for the garnish with the parsley and chives. Sprinkle the mixture over each salad.

VARIATION
This is equally good made with halibut, monkfish or cod. For a change, try it with a dressing of home-made mayonnaise mixed with capers.

WARM SWORDFISH AND ROCKET SALAD

SWORDFISH IS ROBUST ENOUGH TO TAKE THE SHARP FLAVOURS OF ROCKET AND PECORINO CHEESE. IF YOU CAN'T FIND PECORINO, USE A GOOD PARMESAN INSTEAD. YOU COULD SUBSTITUTE MARLIN OR SHARK FOR THE SWORDFISH, IF YOU LIKE.

SERVES FOUR

INGREDIENTS

  4 swordfish steaks, about
    175g/6oz each
  75ml/5 tbsp extra virgin olive oil,
    plus extra for serving
  juice of 1 lemon
  30ml/2 tbsp finely chopped
    fresh parsley
  115g/4oz rocket (arugula) leaves,
    stalks snipped off
  115g/4oz Pecorino cheese
  salt and ground black pepper

1 Lay the swordfish steaks in a dish. Mix 60ml/4 tbsp of the olive oil with the lemon juice. Pour over the fish. Season, sprinkle on the parsley and turn the fish to coat, cover with clear film (plastic wrap) and marinate for 10 minutes.

2 Heat a ridged griddle pan or the grill (broiler) until very hot. Take the fish out of the marinade and pat it dry with kitchen paper. Grill (broil) for 2–3 minutes on each side until the swordfish is just cooked through, but still juicy.

3 Meanwhile, put the rocket leaves in a bowl and season with a little salt and plenty of pepper. Add the remaining 15ml/1 tbsp olive oil and toss well. Shave the Pecorino over the top.

4 Place the swordfish steaks on four individual plates and arrange a little pile of salad on each steak. Serve extra olive oil separately so it may be drizzled over the swordfish.

VARIATION
Tuna or shark steaks would be equally good in this recipe.

PROVENÇAL AIOLI <u>WITH</u> SALT COD

THIS SUBSTANTIAL SALAD CONSTITUTES A MEAL ON ITS OWN AND IS ONE OF THE NICEST DISHES FOR SUMMER ENTERTAINING. VARY THE VEGETABLES ACCORDING TO WHAT IS IN SEASON; IF YOU LIKE RAW VEGETABLES, INCLUDE RADISHES, YELLOW PEPPER AND CELERY FOR COLOUR CONTRAST.

SERVES SIX

INGREDIENTS
- 1kg/2¼lb salt cod, soaked overnight in water to cover
- 1 fresh bouquet garni
- 18 small new potatoes, scrubbed
- 1 large fresh mint sprig, torn
- 225g/8oz green beans, trimmed
- 225g/8oz broccoli florets
- 6 hard-boiled (hard-cooked) eggs
- 12 baby carrots, with leaves if possible, scrubbed
- 1 large red (bell) pepper, seeded and cut into strips
- 2 fennel bulbs, cut into strips
- 18 red or yellow cherry tomatoes
- 6 large whole cooked prawns (shrimp) or langoustines, in the shell, to garnish (optional)

For the aioli
- 600ml/1 pint/2½ cups home-made mayonnaise
- 2 fat garlic cloves, (or more if you are feeling brave), crushed
- cayenne pepper

1 Drain the cod and put it into a shallow pan. Pour in barely enough water to cover the fish and add the bouquet garni. Bring to the boil, then cover and poach very gently for about 10 minutes, until the fish flakes easily when tested with the tip of a sharp knife. Drain and set aside until required.

2 Cook the potatoes with the mint in a pan of lightly salted boiling water until just tender. Drain and set aside. Cook the beans and broccoli in separate pans of lightly salted boiling water for about 3–5 minutes. They should still be very crisp. Refresh under cold water and drain again, then set aside.

3 Remove the skin from the cod and break the flesh into large flakes. Shell and halve the eggs lengthways.

4 Pile the cod in the middle of a large serving platter and arrange the eggs and all the vegetables around the edges or randomly. Garnish with the prawns or langoustines if you are using them.

5 To make the aioli, put the home-made mayonnaise in a bowl and stir in the crushed garlic and cayenne pepper to taste. Serve in individual bowls or one large bowl to hand around.

SMOKED EEL AND CHICORY SALAD

SMOKED EEL HAS BECOME INCREASINGLY POPULAR RECENTLY AND IS SEEN ON SOME OF THE MOST SOPHISTICATED TABLES. IT TASTES MARVELLOUS IN A SALAD WITH A REFRESHING CITRUS DRESSING.

SERVES FOUR

INGREDIENTS
  450g/1lb smoked eel fillets, skinned
  2 large heads of chicory (belgian
    endive), separated
  4 radicchio leaves
  flat leaf parsley leaves, to garnish
For the citrus dressing
  1 lemon
  1 orange
  5ml/1 tsp sugar
  5ml/1 tsp Dijon mustard
  90ml/6 tbsp sunflower oil
  15ml/1 tbsp chopped fresh parsley
  salt and ground black pepper

VARIATION
This salad can also be made with other hot-smoked fish such as trout or mackerel.

1 Cut the eel fillets diagonally into 8 pieces. Make the dressing. Using a zester, carefully remove the rind in strips from the lemon and the orange. Squeeze the juice of both fruit. Set the lemon juice aside and pour the orange juice into a small pan. Stir in the rinds and sugar. Bring to the boil and reduce by half. Leave to cool.

2 Whisk the Dijon mustard, reserved lemon juice and the sunflower oil together in a bowl. Add the orange juice mixture, then stir in the chopped fresh parsley. Season to taste with salt and ground black pepper and whisk again.

3 Arrange the chicory leaves in a circle on individual plates, with the pointed ends radiating outwards like the spokes of a wheel. Take the radicchio leaves and arrange them on the plates, between the chicory leaves.

4 Drizzle a little of the dressing over the leaves and place four pieces of eel in a star-shape in the middle. Garnish with the parsley leaves and serve. Offer the remaining dressing separately.

SKATE WITH BITTER SALAD LEAVES

SKATE HAS A DELICIOUSLY SWEET FLAVOUR WHICH CONTRASTS WELL WITH THE BITTERNESS OF SALAD LEAVES SUCH AS ESCAROLE, ROCKET, FRISÉE AND RADICCHIO. SERVE WITH TOASTED FRENCH BREAD.

SERVES FOUR

INGREDIENTS
  800g/1¾lb skate wings
  15ml/1 tbsp white wine vinegar
  4 black peppercorns
  1 fresh thyme sprig
  175g/6oz bag of ready-prepared
    bitter salad leaves, such as frisée,
    rocket (arugula), radicchio, escarole
    and lamb's lettuce (corn salad)
  1 orange
  2 tomatoes, peeled, seeded
    and diced
For the dressing
  15ml/1 tbsp white wine vinegar
  45ml/3 tbsp olive oil
  2 shallots, finely chopped
  salt and ground black pepper

1 Put the skate wings into a large shallow pan, cover with cold water and add the vinegar, peppercorns and thyme. Bring to the boil, then poach the fish gently for 8–10 minutes, until the flesh comes away easily from the bones.

2 Meanwhile, make the dressing. Whisk the vinegar, olive oil and shallots together in a bowl. Season to taste. Tip the salad leaves into a bowl, pour over the dressing and toss well.

3 Using a zester, remove the outer rind from the orange, then peel it, removing all the pith. Slice into thin rounds.

4 When the skate is cooked, flake the flesh and mix it into the salad. Add the orange rind shreds, the orange slices and tomatoes, toss gently and serve.

COOK'S TIP
When peeling the orange, take care not to include any of the bitter white pith.

WARM MONKFISH SALAD

MONKFISH HAS A MATCHLESS FLAVOUR AND BENEFITS FROM BEING COOKED SIMPLY. TEAMING IT WITH WILTED BABY SPINACH AND TOASTED PINE NUTS IS INSPIRATIONAL.

3 Make the dressing by whisking all the ingredients together until smooth and creamy. Pour the dressing into a small pan, season to taste with salt and pepper and heat gently.

4 Heat the oil and butter in a ridged griddle pan or frying pan until sizzling. Add the fish; sauté for 20–30 seconds on each side.

SERVES FOUR

INGREDIENTS

   2 monkfish fillets, about
     350g/12oz each
   25g/1oz/¼ cup pine nuts
   15ml/1 tbsp olive oil
   15g/½oz/1 tbsp butter
   225g/8oz baby spinach leaves,
     washed and stalks removed
   salt and ground black pepper
For the dressing
   5ml/1 tsp Dijon mustard
   5ml/1 tsp sherry vinegar
   60ml/4 tbsp olive oil
   1 garlic clove, crushed

VARIATION
Substitute salad leaves for the spinach.

1 Holding the knife at a slight angle, cut each monkfish fillet into 12 diagonal slices. Season lightly and set aside.

2 Heat an empty frying pan, put in the pine nuts and shake them about for a while, until golden brown. Do not burn. Transfer to a plate; set aside.

5 Put the spinach leaves in a large bowl and pour over the warm dressing. Sprinkle on the toasted pine nuts, reserving a few, and toss together well. Divide the dressed spinach leaves among four serving plates and arrange the monkfish slices on top. Sprinkle the reserved pine nuts on top and serve.

ASPARAGUS AND LANGOUSTINE SALAD

FOR A REALLY EXTRAVAGANT TREAT, YOU COULD MAKE THIS ATTRACTIVE SALAD WITH MEDALLIONS OF LOBSTER. FOR A CHEAPER VERSION, USE LARGE PRAWNS, ALLOWING SIX PER SERVING.

SERVES FOUR

INGREDIENTS
    16 langoustines
    16 fresh asparagus spears, trimmed
    2 carrots
    30ml/2 tbsp olive oil
    1 garlic clove, peeled
    15ml/1 tbsp chopped fresh tarragon
    4 fresh tarragon sprigs and some
        chopped, to garnish
For the dressing
    30ml/2 tbsp tarragon vinegar
    120ml/4fl oz/½ cup olive oil
    salt and ground black pepper

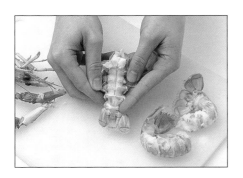

1 Shell the langoustines and keep the discarded parts for stock. Set aside.

2 Steam the asparagus over boiling salted water until just tender, but still a little crisp. Refresh under cold water, drain and place in a shallow dish.

3 Peel the carrots and cut into fine julienne shreds. Cook in a pan of lightly salted boiling water for about 3 minutes, until tender but still crunchy. Drain, refresh under cold water, drain again. Place in the dish with the asparagus.

4 Make the dressing. Whisk the vinegar with the oil in a jug (pitcher). Season to taste. Pour over the asparagus and carrots and leave to marinate.

5 Heat the oil with the garlic in a frying pan until very hot. Add the langoustines and sauté quickly until just heated through. Discard the garlic.

6 Cut the asparagus spears in half and arrange on four individual plates with the carrots. Drizzle over the dressing left in the dish and top each portion with four langoustine tails. Top with the tarragon sprigs and sprinkle the chopped tarragon on top. Serve.

COOK'S TIP
Most of the langoustines we buy have been cooked at sea; this is necessary because the flesh deteriorates rapidly after death. Bear this in mind when you cook the shellfish. Because they have already been cooked, they will need only to be lightly sautéed until heated through. If you are lucky enough to buy live langoustines, kill them quickly by immersing them in boiling water, then sauté until cooked through.

EVERYDAY MAIN COURSES

Healthy everyday eating becomes a treat when you serve interesting, affordable fish dishes. Quick to prepare, low in fat and packed with nutrients, fish makes the perfect family meal. From simple-to-cook old favourites, such as Fish Pie and Salmon Fish Cakes, to Trout with Tamarind and Chilli Sauce, and Green Fish Curry, there's a dish to suit everyone, even those who profess not to like fish. You will be surprised how little time it takes to make these delicious everyday meals.

SALMON FISH CAKES

THE SECRET OF A GOOD FISH CAKE IS TO MAKE IT WITH FRESHLY PREPARED FISH AND POTATOES, HOME-MADE BREADCRUMBS AND PLENTY OF INTERESTING SEASONING.

SERVES FOUR

INGREDIENTS

  450g/1lb cooked salmon fillet
  450g/1lb freshly cooked
    potatoes, mashed
  25g/1oz/2 tbsp butter, melted
  10ml/2 tsp wholegrain mustard
  15ml/1 tbsp each chopped fresh dill
    and chopped fresh parsley
  grated rind and juice of ½ lemon
  15ml/1 tbsp plain (all-purpose) flour
  1 egg, lightly beaten
  150g/5oz/1¼ cups dried breadcrumbs
  60ml/4 tbsp sunflower oil
  salt and ground black pepper
  rocket (arugula) and chives, to garnish
  lemon wedges, to serve

1 Flake the cooked salmon, discarding any skin and bones. Put it in a bowl with the mashed potato, melted butter and wholegrain mustard, and mix well. Stir in the dill and parsley and lemon rind and juice. Season to taste with salt and pepper.

2 Divide the mixture into 8 portions and shape each into a ball, then flatten into a thick disc. Dip the fish cakes first in flour, then in egg and finally in breadcrumbs, making sure that they are evenly coated.

3 Heat the oil in a frying pan until it is very hot. Fry the fish cakes in batches until golden brown and crisp all over. As each batch is ready, drain on kitchen paper and keep hot. Garnish with rocket leaves and chives and serve with lemon wedges.

COOK'S TIP

Almost any fresh white or hot-smoked fish is suitable; smoked cod and haddock are particularly good.

CRAB CAKES

Unlike fish cakes, crab cakes are bound with egg and mayonnaise or tartare sauce instead of potatoes, which makes them light in texture. If you like, they can be grilled instead of fried; brush with a little oil first.

SERVES FOUR

INGREDIENTS
   450g/1lb mixed brown and white
      crab meat
   30ml/2 tbsp mayonnaise or
      tartare sauce
   2.5–5ml/½–1 tsp mustard powder
   1 egg, lightly beaten
   Tabasco sauce
   45ml/3 tbsp chopped fresh parsley
   4 spring onions (scallions), finely
      chopped (optional)
   50–75g/2–3oz/½–¾ cup dried
      breadcrumbs, preferably home-made
   sunflower oil, for frying
   salt, ground black pepper and
      cayenne pepper
   chopped spring onions (scallions), to
      garnish
   red onion marmalade, to serve

1 Put the crab meat in a bowl and stir in the mayonnaise or tartare sauce, with the mustard and egg. Season with Tabasco, salt, pepper and cayenne.

2 Stir in the parsley, spring onions, if using, and 50g/2oz/½ cup of the breadcrumbs. The mixture should be just firm enough to hold together; depending on how much brown crab meat there is, you may need to add some more breadcrumbs.

3 Divide the mixture into 8 portions, roll each into a ball and flatten slightly to make a thick flat disc. Spread out the crab cakes on a platter and put in the refrigerator for 30 minutes before frying.

4 Pour the oil into a shallow pan to a depth of about 5mm/¼in. Fry the crab cakes in two batches until golden brown all over. Drain on kitchen paper and keep hot. Serve with a spring onion garnish and red onion marmalade.

SARDINE FRITTATA

IT MAY SEEM ODD TO COOK SARDINES IN AN OMELETTE, BUT THEY ARE SURPRISINGLY DELICIOUS THIS WAY. FROZEN SARDINES ARE FINE FOR THIS DISH. SERVE THE FRITTATA WITH CRISP SAUTÉED POTATOES AND THINLY SLICED CUCUMBER CRESCENTS.

SERVES FOUR

INGREDIENTS
    4 fat sardines, cleaned, filleted and
       with heads removed, thawed
       if frozen
    juice of 1 lemon
    45ml/3 tbsp olive oil
    6 large (US extra large) eggs
    30ml/2 tbsp chopped fresh parsley
    30ml/2 tbsp chopped fresh chives
    1 garlic clove, chopped
    salt, ground black pepper
       and paprika

1 Open out the sardines and sprinkle the fish with lemon juice, a little salt and paprika. Heat 15ml/1 tbsp olive oil in a frying pan and fry the sardines for about 1–2 minutes on each side to seal them. Drain on kitchen paper, trim off the tails and set aside until required.

2 Separate the eggs. In a bowl, whisk the yolks lightly with the parsley, chives and a little salt and pepper. Beat the whites in a separate bowl with a pinch of salt until fairly stiff. Preheat the grill (broiler) to medium-high.

3 Heat the remaining olive oil in a large frying pan, add the garlic and cook over a low heat until just golden. Gently mix together the egg yolks and whites and ladle half the mixture into the pan. Cook gently until just beginning to set on the base, then lay the sardines on the frittata and sprinkle lightly with paprika. Pour over the remaining egg mixture and cook gently until the frittata has browned underneath and is beginning to set on the top.

4 Put the pan under the grill and cook until the top of the frittata is golden. Cut into wedges and serve immediately.

COOK'S TIP

It is important to use a frying pan with a handle that can safely be used under the grill (broiler). If your frying pan has a wooden handle, protect it with foil.

FISH PIE

FISH PIE CAN BE VARIED TO SUIT YOUR TASTE AND POCKET. THIS IS A SIMPLE VERSION, BUT YOU COULD ADD PRAWNS OR HARD-BOILED EGGS, OR MIX THE POTATO TOPPING WITH SPRING ONIONS.

SERVES FOUR

INGREDIENTS

   450g/1lb cod or haddock fillets
   225g/8oz smoked cod fillets
   300ml/½ pint/1¼ cups milk
   ½ lemon, sliced
   1 bay leaf
   1 fresh thyme sprig
   4–5 black peppercorns
   50g/2oz/¼ cup butter
   25g/1oz/¼ cup plain (all-purpose) flour
   30ml/2 tbsp chopped fresh parsley
   5ml/1 tsp anchovy essence (paste)
   150g/5oz/2 cups shiitake or chestnut
     mushrooms, sliced
   salt, ground black pepper and
     cayenne pepper
For the topping
   450g/1lb potatoes, cooked and
     mashed with milk
   50g/2oz/¼ cup butter
   2 tomatoes, sliced
   25g/1oz/¼ cup grated Cheddar
     cheese (optional)

1 Put the fish skin-side down in a shallow pan. Add the milk, lemon slices, bay leaf, thyme and peppercorns. Bring to the boil, then lower the heat and poach gently for about 5 minutes, until just cooked. Strain off and reserve the milk. Remove the fish skin and flake the flesh, discarding any bones.

2 Melt half the butter in a small pan, stir in the flour and cook gently for 1 minute. Add the milk and boil, whisking, until smooth and creamy. Stir in the parsley and anchovy essence and season to taste.

3 Heat the remaining butter in a frying pan, add the sliced mushrooms and sauté until tender. Season and add to the flaked fish. Mix the sauce into the fish and stir gently to combine. Transfer the mixture to an ovenproof casserole.

4 Preheat the oven to 200°C/400°F/ Gas 6. Beat the mashed potato with the butter until very creamy. Season, then spread the topping evenly over the fish. Fork up the surface and arrange the sliced tomatoes around the edge. Sprinkle the exposed topping with the grated cheese, if using.

5 Bake for 20–25 minutes, until the topping is lightly browned.

VARIATION
Instead of using plain mashed potatoes for the topping, try a mixture of mashed potato and mashed swede (rutabaga) or sweet potato.

SALMON AND PRAWN TART

THIS TART IS UNUSUAL BECAUSE IT IS MADE WITH RAW SALMON, WHICH MEANS THAT THE FISH STAYS MOIST. COOKING IT THIS WAY GIVES A LOVELY SUCCULENT RESULT. THIS VERSATILE DISH MAY BE SERVED HOT WITH VEGETABLES OR COOL WITH MIXED SALAD LEAVES AND TOMATO WEDGES.

SERVES SIX

INGREDIENTS

  350g/12oz shortcrust (unsweetened)
    pastry, thawed if frozen
  225g/8oz salmon fillet, skinned
  225g/8oz/2 cups cooked peeled
    prawns (shrimp)
  2 eggs, plus 2 egg yolks
  150ml/¼ pint/⅔ cup
    whipping cream
  200ml/7fl oz/scant 1 cup milk
  15ml/1 tbsp chopped fresh dill
  salt, ground black pepper and paprika
  lime slices, tomato wedges and sprigs
    of dill, to garnish

VARIATION

For a more economical version of this flan, omit the prawns (shrimp) and use some extra salmon instead, or use a mixture of salmon and white fish.

1 Roll out the pastry on a floured work surface and use it to line a 20cm/8in quiche dish or tin (pan). Prick the base all over and mark the edges with the tines of the fork. It need not be too neat. Chill for about 30 minutes. Meanwhile, preheat the oven to 180°C/ 350°F/Gas 4. Bake the pastry case (shell) for about 30 minutes, until golden brown. Reduce the oven temperature to 160°C/325°F/Gas 3.

2 Cut the salmon into 2cm/¾in cubes. Arrange the salmon and prawns evenly in the pastry case. Dust with paprika.

3 In a bowl, beat together the eggs and yolks, cream, milk and dill and season to taste. Pour over the salmon and prawns. Bake for about 30 minutes, until the filling is just set. Serve hot or at room temperature, garnished with lime slices, tomato wedges and dill.

COCONUT BAKED SNAPPER

ADDING A COUPLE OF FRESH RED CHILLIES TO THE MARINADE GIVES THIS DISH A REALLY SPICY FLAVOUR. SERVE THE BAKED SNAPPER WITH PLAIN BOILED RICE.

SERVES FOUR

INGREDIENTS

  1 snapper, about 1kg/2¼lb, scaled
    and cleaned
  400ml/14fl oz/1⅔ cups coconut milk
  105ml/7 tbsp dry white wine
  juice of 1 lime
  45ml/3 tbsp light soy sauce
  1–2 fresh red chillies, seeded and
    finely sliced (optional)
  60ml/4 tbsp chopped fresh parsley
  45ml/3 tbsp chopped fresh
    coriander (cilantro)
  salt and ground black pepper

COOK'S TIP

Any type of snapper or trout can be used for this recipe. If you like, use one small fish per person.

1 Lay the snapper in an ovenproof shallow dish and season with a little salt and plenty of pepper. Mix together the coconut milk, wine, lime juice, soy sauce and chillies, if using. Stir in the herbs and pour over the fish. Cover with clear film (plastic wrap) and marinate in the refrigerator for about 4 hours, turning the fish over halfway through.

2 Preheat the oven to 190°C/375°F/ Gas 5. Take the fish out of the marinade and wrap loosely in foil, spooning over the marinade before sealing the parcel. Support the fish on a clean dish and bake for 30–40 minutes, until the flesh comes away easily from the bone.

FRIED PLAICE WITH TOMATO SAUCE

THIS SIMPLE DISH IS PERENNIALLY POPULAR WITH CHILDREN. IT WORKS EQUALLY WELL WITH LEMON SOLE OR DABS (THESE DO NOT NEED SKINNING), OR FILLETS OF HADDOCK AND WHITING.

SERVES FOUR

INGREDIENTS

25g/1oz/¼ cup plain (all-purpose) flour
2 eggs, beaten
75g/3oz/¾ cup dried breadcrumbs, preferably home-made
4 small plaice or flounder, skinned
15g/½oz/1 tbsp butter
15ml/1 tbsp sunflower oil
salt and ground black pepper
1 lemon, quartered, to serve
fresh basil leaves, to garnish

For the tomato sauce

30ml/2 tbsp olive oil
1 red onion, finely chopped
1 garlic clove, finely chopped
400g/14oz can chopped tomatoes
15ml/1 tbsp tomato purée (paste)
15ml/1 tbsp torn fresh basil leaves

1 First make the tomato sauce. Heat the olive oil in a large pan, add the finely chopped onion and garlic and cook gently for about 5 minutes, until softened and pale golden. Stir in the chopped tomatoes and tomato purée and simmer for 20–30 minutes, stirring occasionally. Season with salt and pepper and stir in the basil.

2 Spread out the flour in a shallow dish, pour the beaten eggs into another and spread out the breadcrumbs in a third. Season the fish with salt and pepper.

3 Hold a fish in your left hand and dip it first in flour, then in egg and finally in the breadcrumbs, patting the crumbs on with your dry right hand.

4 Heat the butter and oil in a frying pan until foaming. Fry the fish one at a time in the hot fat for about 5 minutes on each side, until golden brown and cooked through, but still juicy in the middle. Drain on kitchen paper and keep hot while you fry the rest. Serve with lemon wedges and the tomato sauce, garnished with basil leaves.

COD CARAMBA

THIS COLOURFUL MEXICAN DISH, WITH ITS CONTRASTING CRUNCHY TOPPING AND TENDER FISH FILLING, CAN BE MADE WITH ANY ECONOMICAL WHITE FISH SUCH AS COLEY OR HADDOCK.

SERVES FOUR TO SIX

INGREDIENTS
   450g/1lb cod fillets
   225g/8oz smoked cod fillets
   300ml/½ pint/1¼ cups fish stock
   50g/2oz/¼ cup butter
   1 onion, sliced
   2 garlic cloves, crushed
   1 green and 1 red (bell) pepper,
      seeded and diced
   2 courgettes (zucchini), diced
   115g/4oz/⅔ cup drained canned or
      thawed frozen sweetcorn kernels
   2 tomatoes, peeled and chopped
   juice of 1 lime
   Tabasco sauce
   salt, ground black pepper and
      cayenne pepper
For the topping
   75g/3oz tortilla chips
   50g/2oz/½ cup grated
      Cheddar cheese
   coriander (cilantro) sprigs, to garnish
   lime wedges, to serve

1 Lay the fish in a shallow pan and pour over the fish stock. Bring to the boil, lower the heat, cover and poach for about 8 minutes, until the flesh flakes easily when tested with the tip of a sharp knife. Leave to cool slightly, then remove the skin and separate the flesh into large flakes. Keep hot.

2 Melt the butter in a pan, add the onion and garlic and cook over a low heat until soft. Add the peppers, stir and cook for 2 minutes. Stir in the courgettes and cook for 3 minutes more, until all the vegetables are tender.

3 Stir in the sweetcorn and tomatoes, then add lime juice and Tabasco to taste. Season with salt, black pepper and cayenne. Cook for a few minutes to heat the corn and tomatoes, then stir in the fish and transfer to a dish that can safely be used under the grill (broiler).

4 Preheat the grill. Make the topping by crushing the tortilla chips, then mixing in the grated cheese. Add cayenne pepper to taste and sprinkle over the fish. Place the dish under the grill until the topping is crisp and brown. Garnish with coriander sprigs and lime wedges.

HERRINGS IN OATMEAL WITH BACON

THIS TRADITIONAL SCOTTISH DISH IS CHEAP AND NUTRITIOUS. FOR EASE OF EATING, BONE THE HERRINGS BEFORE COATING THEM IN THE OATMEAL. IF YOU DON'T LIKE HERRINGS, USE TROUT OR MACKEREL INSTEAD. FOR EXTRA COLOUR AND FLAVOUR, SERVE WITH GRILLED TOMATOES.

SERVES FOUR

INGREDIENTS

    115–150g/4–5oz/1–1¼ cups
      medium oatmeal
    10ml/2 tsp mustard powder
    4 herrings, about 225g/8oz each,
      cleaned, boned, heads and
      tails removed
    30ml/2 tbsp sunflower oil
    8 rindless streaky (fatty) bacon
      rashers (strips)
    salt and ground black pepper
    lemon wedges, to serve

COOK'S TIPS

• Use tongs to turn the herrings so as not to dislodge the oatmeal.
• Cook the herrings two at a time.
• Don't overcrowd the frying pan.

1 In a shallow dish, mix together the oatmeal and mustard powder with salt and pepper. Press the herrings into the mixture, one at a time, to coat them thickly on both sides. Shake off the excess oatmeal mixture and set the herrings aside.

2 Heat the oil in a large frying pan and fry the bacon until crisp. Drain on kitchen paper and keep hot.

3 Put the herrings into the pan and fry them for 3–4 minutes on each side, until crisp and golden brown. Serve the herrings with the streaky bacon rashers and lemon wedges.

SKATE WITH BLACK BUTTER

SKATE CAN BE QUITE INEXPENSIVE, AND THIS CLASSIC DISH IS PERFECT FOR A FAMILY SUPPER. SERVE IT WITH STEAMED LEEKS AND PLAIN BOILED POTATOES.

SERVES FOUR

INGREDIENTS

    4 skate wings, about
      225g/8oz each
    60ml/4 tbsp red wine vinegar
      or malt vinegar
    30ml/2 tbsp drained capers in
      vinegar, chopped if large
    30ml/2 tbsp chopped fresh parsley
    150g/5oz/⅔ cup butter
    salt and ground black pepper

COOK'S TIP

Despite the title of the recipe, the butter should be a rich golden brown. It should never be allowed to blacken, or it will taste unpleasantly bitter.

1 Put the skate wings in a large, shallow pan, cover with cold water and add a pinch of salt and 15ml/1 tbsp of the red wine or malt vinegar.

2 Bring to the boil, skim the surface, then lower the heat and simmer gently for about 10–12 minutes, until the skate flesh comes away from the bone easily. Carefully drain the skate and peel off the skin.

3 Transfer the skate to a warmed serving dish, season with salt and pepper and sprinkle over the capers and parsley. Keep hot.

4 In a small pan, heat the butter until it foams and turns a rich nutty brown. Pour it over the skate. Pour the remaining vinegar into the pan and boil until reduced by about two-thirds. Drizzle over the skate and serve.

TROUT WITH TAMARIND AND CHILLI SAUCE

TROUT IS A VERY ECONOMICAL FISH, BUT CAN TASTE RATHER BLAND. THIS SPICY THAI-INSPIRED SAUCE REALLY GIVES IT A ZING. IF YOU LIKE YOUR FOOD VERY SPICY, ADD AN EXTRA CHILLI.

SERVES FOUR

INGREDIENTS

    4 trout, about 350g/12oz
      each, cleaned
    6 spring onions (scallions), sliced
    60ml/4 tbsp soy sauce
    15ml/1 tbsp stir-fry oil
    30ml/2 tbsp chopped fresh
      coriander (cilantro)
For the sauce
    50g/2oz tamarind pulp
    105ml/7 tbsp boiling water
    2 shallots, roughly chopped
    1 fresh red chilli, seeded and chopped
    1cm/½in piece fresh root ginger,
      peeled and chopped
    5ml/1 tsp soft brown sugar
    45ml/3 tbsp Thai fish sauce (*nam pla*)

1 Slash the trout diagonally four or five times on each side with a sharp knife and place in a shallow dish.

2 Fill the cavities with spring onions and douse each fish with soy sauce. Carefully turn the fish over to coat both sides with the sauce. Sprinkle on any remaining spring onions and set aside until required.

3 Make the sauce. Put the tamarind pulp in a small bowl and pour on the boiling water. Mash with a fork until soft. Tip into a food processor or blender, add the shallots, fresh chilli, ginger, sugar and fish sauce and process to a coarse pulp.

4 Heat the stir-fry oil in a large frying pan or wok and fry the trout, one at a time if necessary, for about 5 minutes on each side, until the skin is crisp and browned and the flesh cooked. Put on warmed plates and spoon over some sauce. Sprinkle with the coriander and serve with the remaining sauce.

GREEN FISH CURRY

ANY FIRM-FLESHED FISH CAN BE USED FOR THIS DELICIOUS CURRY, WHICH GAINS ITS RICH COLOUR FROM A MIXTURE OF FRESH HERBS; TRY EXOTICS, SUCH AS MAHI MAHI, HOKI OR SWORDFISH, OR HUMBLER FISH, SUCH AS COLEY. SERVE IT WITH BASMATI OR THAI FRAGRANT RICE AND LIME WEDGES.

SERVES FOUR

INGREDIENTS

   4 garlic cloves, roughly chopped
   5cm/2in piece fresh root ginger,
     peeled and roughly chopped
   2 fresh green chillies, seeded and
     roughly chopped
   grated rind and juice of 1 lime
   5–10ml/1–2 tsp shrimp paste (optional)
   5ml/1 tsp coriander seeds
   5ml/1 tsp five-spice powder
   75ml/5 tbsp sesame oil
   2 red onions, finely chopped
   900g/2lb hoki fillets, skinned
   400ml/14fl oz/1⅔ cups coconut milk
   45ml/3 tbsp Thai fish sauce (*nam pla*)
   50g/2oz fresh coriander
     (cilantro) leaves
   50g/2oz fresh mint leaves
   50g/2oz fresh basil leaves
   6 spring onions, chopped
   150ml/¼ pint/⅔ cup sunflower or
     groundnut (peanut) oil
   sliced fresh green chilli and chopped
     fresh coriander (cilantro), to garnish
   cooked basmati or Thai fragrant rice
     and lime wedges, to serve

1 First make the curry paste. Combine the garlic, fresh root ginger, green chillies, the lime juice and shrimp paste (if using) in a food processor. Add the coriander seeds and five-spice powder, with half the sesame oil. Process to a fine paste, then set aside until required.

2 Heat a wok or large shallow pan and pour in the remaining sesame oil. When it is hot, stir-fry the red onions over a high heat for 2 minutes. Add the fish and stir-fry for 1–2 minutes to seal the fillets on all sides.

3 Lift out the red onions and fish and put them on a plate. Add the curry paste to the wok or pan and fry for 1 minute, stirring. Return the hoki fillets and red onions to the wok or pan, pour in the coconut milk and bring to the boil. Lower the heat, add the fish sauce and simmer for 5–7 minutes, until the fish is cooked through.

4 Meanwhile, process the herbs, spring onions, lime rind and oil in a food processor to a coarse paste. Stir into the fish curry. Garnish with chilli and coriander and serve with rice and lime wedges.

KEDGEREE

THIS CLASSIC DISH ORIGINATED IN INDIA. IT IS BEST MADE WITH BASMATI RICE, WHICH GOES WELL WITH THE MILD CURRY FLAVOUR, BUT LONG GRAIN RICE WILL DO. FOR A COLOURFUL GARNISH, ADD SOME FINELY SLICED RED ONION AND A LITTLE RED ONION MARMALADE.

SERVES FOUR

INGREDIENTS
  450g/1lb undyed smoked
    haddock fillet
  750ml/1¼ pints/3 cups milk
  2 bay leaves
  ½ lemon, sliced
  50g/2oz/¼ cup butter
  1 onion, chopped
  2.5ml/½ tsp ground turmeric
  5ml/1 tsp mild Madras curry powder
  2 green cardamom pods
  350g/12oz/1¾ cups basmati or long
    grain rice, washed and drained
  4 hard-boiled eggs (hard-cooked),
    roughly chopped
  150ml/¼ pint/⅔ cup single (light)
    cream (optional)
  30ml/2 tbsp chopped fresh parsley
  salt and ground black pepper

1 Put the haddock in a shallow pan and add the milk, bay leaves and lemon slices. Poach gently for 8–10 minutes, until the haddock flakes easily when tested with the tip of a sharp knife. Strain the milk into a jug (pitcher), discarding the bay leaves and lemon slices. Remove the skin from the haddock and flake the flesh into large pieces. Keep hot until required.

2 Melt the butter in the pan, add the onion and cook over a low heat for about 3 minutes, until softened. Stir in the turmeric, the curry powder and cardamom pods and cook for 1 minute.

3 Add the rice, stirring to coat it well with the butter. Pour in the reserved milk, stir and bring to the boil. Lower the heat and simmer the rice for 10–12 minutes, until all the milk has been absorbed and the rice is tender. Season to taste, going easy on the salt.

4 Gently stir in the fish and hard-boiled eggs, with the cream, if using. Sprinkle with the parsley and serve.

VARIATION
Use smoked and poached fresh salmon for a delicious change from haddock.

GRILLED MACKEREL <u>WITH</u> SPICY DHAL

OILY FISH LIKE MACKEREL ARE CHEAP AND NUTRITIOUS. THEY ARE COMPLEMENTED BY A TART OR SOUR ACCOMPANIMENT, LIKE THESE TAMARIND-FLAVOURED LENTILS. SERVE WITH CHOPPED FRESH TOMATOES, ONION SALAD AND FLAT BREAD.

<u>SERVES FOUR</u>

INGREDIENTS

   250g/9oz/1 cup red lentils, or yellow
     split peas (soaked overnight)
   1 litre/1¾ pints/4 cups water
   30ml/2 tbsp sunflower oil
   2.5ml/½ tsp each mustard seeds,
     cumin seeds, fennel seeds, and
     fenugreek or cardamom seeds
   5ml/1 tsp ground turmeric
   3–4 dried red chillies, crumbled
   30ml/2 tbsp tamarind paste
   5ml/1 tsp soft brown sugar
   30ml/2 tbsp chopped fresh
     coriander (cilantro)
   4 mackerel or 8 large sardines
   salt and ground black pepper
   fresh red chilli slices and chopped
     coriander (cilantro), to garnish

1 Rinse the lentils or split peas, drain them thoroughly and put them in a pan. Pour in the water and bring to the boil. Lower the heat, partially cover the pan and simmer for 30–40 minutes, stirring occasionally, until the pulses are tender and soft.

2 Heat the oil in a wok or shallow pan. Add the mustard seeds, then cover and cook for a few seconds, until they pop. Remove the lid, add the rest of the seeds, with the turmeric and chillies and fry for a few more seconds.

3 Stir in the pulses, with salt to taste. Mix well; stir in the tamarind paste and sugar. Bring to the boil, then simmer for 10 minutes, until thick. Stir in the chopped fresh coriander.

4 Meanwhile, clean the fish, then heat a ridged griddle pan or the grill (broiler) until very hot. Make six diagonal slashes on either side of each fish and remove the heads if you like. Season inside and out, then grill (broil) for 5–7 minutes on each side, until the skin is crisp. Serve with the dhal, garnished with red chilli and chopped coriander.

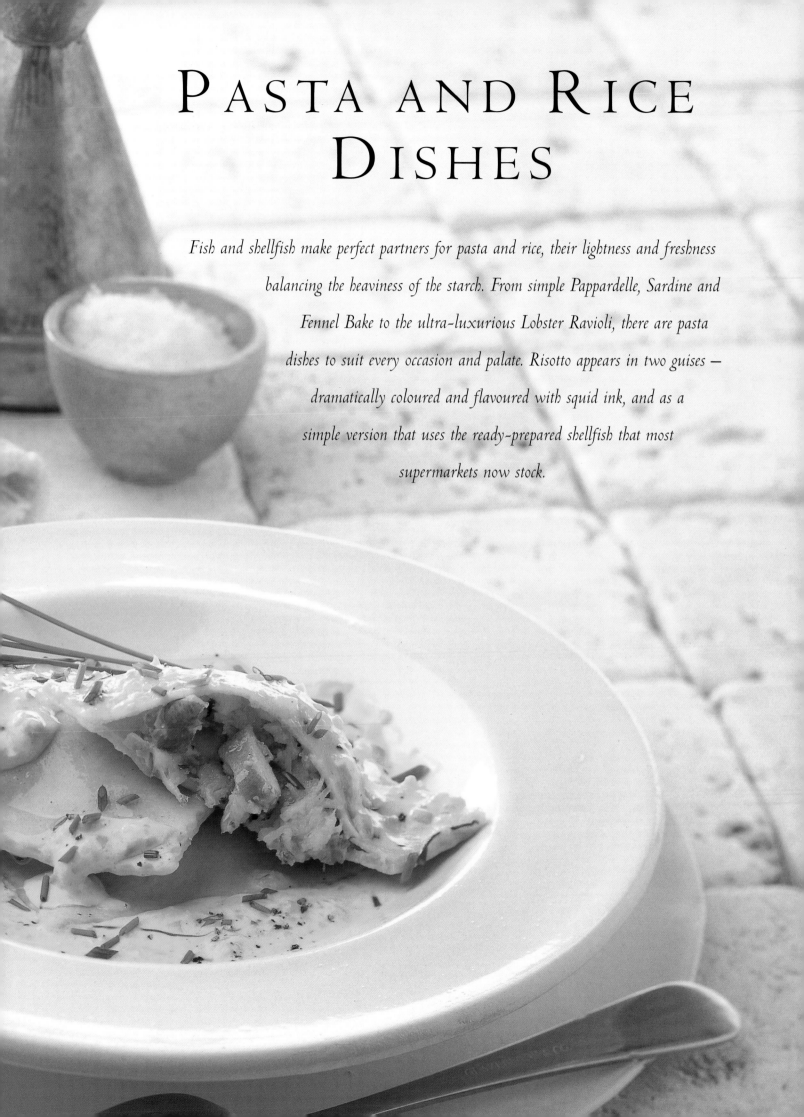

PASTA AND RICE DISHES

Fish and shellfish make perfect partners for pasta and rice, their lightness and freshness balancing the heaviness of the starch. From simple Pappardelle, Sardine and Fennel Bake to the ultra-luxurious Lobster Ravioli, there are pasta dishes to suit every occasion and palate. Risotto appears in two guises — dramatically coloured and flavoured with squid ink, and as a simple version that uses the ready-prepared shellfish that most supermarkets now stock.

SEAFOOD LASAGNE

This dish can be as simple or as elegant as you like. For a dinner party, dress it up with scallops, mussels or prawns and a really generous pinch of saffron in the sauce; for a family supper, use simple fish, such as cod and smoked haddock. The lasagne can be prepared in advance and baked at the last moment.

SERVES EIGHT

INGREDIENTS
  350g/12oz monkfish
  350g/12oz salmon fillet
  350g/12oz undyed smoked haddock
  1 litre/1¾ pints/4 cups milk
  500ml/17fl oz/generous 2 cups
    fish stock
  2 bay leaves or a good pinch of
    saffron threads
  1 small onion, peeled and halved
  75g/3oz/6 tbsp butter, plus extra
    for greasing
  45ml/3 tbsp plain (all-purpose) flour
  150g/5oz/2 cups mushrooms, sliced
  225–300g/8–11oz no-precook or
    fresh lasagne
  60ml/4 tbsp freshly grated
    Parmesan cheese
  salt, ground black pepper, grated
    nutmeg and paprika
  rocket (arugula) leaves, to garnish
For the tomato sauce
  30ml/2 tbsp olive oil
  1 red onion, finely chopped
  1 garlic clove, finely chopped
  400g/14oz can chopped tomatoes
  15ml/1 tbsp tomato purée (paste)
  15ml/1 tbsp torn fresh basil leaves

1 Make the tomato sauce. Heat the oil in a pan and cook the onion and garlic over a low heat for 5 minutes, until softened and golden. Stir in the tomatoes and tomato purée and simmer for 20–30 minutes, stirring occasionally. Season and stir in the basil.

COOK'S TIP
It is preferable to use fresh lasagne, if available. Cook the sheets in a large pan of lightly salted boiling water for 3 minutes. Do not overcrowd the pan or the sheets will stick together.

2 Put all the fish in a shallow flameproof dish or pan with the milk, stock, bay leaves or saffron and onion. Bring to the boil over a moderate heat; poach for 5 minutes, until almost cooked. Leave to cool.

3 When the fish is almost cold, strain it, reserving the liquid. Remove the skin and any bones and flake the flesh.

4 Preheat the oven to 180°C/350°F/ Gas 4. Melt the butter in a pan, stir in the flour; cook for 2 minutes, stirring. Gradually add the poaching liquid and bring to the boil, stirring. Add the mushrooms, cook for 2–3 minutes; season with salt, pepper and nutmeg.

5 Lightly grease a shallow ovenproof dish. Spoon a thin layer of the mushroom sauce over the base of the dish and spread it with a spatula. Stir the fish into the remaining mushroom sauce in the pan.

6 Make a layer of lasagne, then a layer of fish and sauce. Add another layer of lasagne, then spread over all the tomato sauce. Continue to layer the lasagne and fish, finishing with a layer of fish.

7 Sprinkle over the grated Parmesan cheese. Bake for 30–45 minutes, until bubbling and golden. Before serving, sprinkle with paprika and garnish with rocket leaves.

SPAGHETTI AL CARTOCCIO

IN THIS RECIPE, THE COOKING IS FINISHED IN A PAPER PARCEL. WHEN THE PARCEL IS OPENED, THE MOST WONDERFUL AROMA WAFTS OUT. TO SERVE AS AN APPETIZER, BAKE IN TWO LARGER PARCELS.

SERVES FOUR AS A MAIN COURSE,
SIX AS AN APPETIZER

INGREDIENTS
    500g/1¼lb live mussels, scrubbed
      and bearded
    500g/1¼lb small clams, scrubbed
    105ml/7 tbsp dry white wine
    60ml/4 tbsp olive oil
    2 fat garlic cloves, chopped
    2 dried red chillies, crumbled
    200g/7oz squid, cut into rings
    200g/7oz raw peeled prawns (shrimp)
    400g/14oz dried spaghetti
    30ml/2 tbsp chopped fresh parsley
    5ml/1 tsp chopped fresh oregano or
      2.5ml/½ tsp dried
    salt and ground black pepper
For the tomato sauce
    30ml/2 tbsp olive oil
    1 red onion, finely chopped
    1 garlic clove, finely chopped
    400g/14oz can chopped tomatoes
    15ml/1 tbsp tomato purée (paste)
    15ml/1 tbsp torn fresh basil leaves

1 Make the tomato sauce. Heat the oil in a pan and cook the onion and garlic over a low heat for 5 minutes. Stir in the tomatoes and tomato purée and simmer for 20–30 minutes, stirring occasionally. Season and add the basil.

2 Put the mussels, clams and wine in a large pan and bring to the boil. Put on the lid and shake the pan until all the shells have opened. Discard any that remain closed. Remove most of the mussels and clams from the shells, leaving about a dozen of each in the shell. Strain the juices and set aside.

3 Heat the olive oil in a frying pan, add the garlic and cook until lightly coloured. Add the chillies, then add the squid and prawns and sauté for 2–3 minutes, until the squid is opaque and the prawns have turned pink. Add the shellfish and their reserved juices, then stir in the tomato sauce. Set aside.

4 Preheat the oven to 240°C/475°F/ Gas 9 or the grill (broiler) to hot. Cook the spaghetti in a pan of lightly salted boiling water for about 12 minutes or until it is just tender. Drain very thoroughly, then return to the clean pan and stir in the shellfish sauce, tossing to coat all the strands of spaghetti. Stir in the parsley and oregano, with some seasoning.

5 Cut out four 25cm/10in square pieces of greaseproof (waxed) paper. Put a quarter of the spaghetti mixture into the middle of one piece and fold up the edges, pleating them to make a secure bag. Seal the sides first, then blow gently into the top to fill the bag with air. Fold over the top to seal. Make another three parcels with the rest of the spaghetti mixture.

6 Place the parcels on a baking sheet and cook in the hot oven or under the grill until the paper is browned and slightly charred at the edges. Transfer the parcels to serving plates and open them at the table so that you can enjoy the wonderful aromas.

PAPPARDELLE, SARDINE AND FENNEL BAKE

PAPPARDELLE ARE WIDE, FLAT NOODLES. THEY ARE PERFECT FOR THIS SICILIAN RECIPE. IF YOU CAN'T FIND THEM, ANY WIDE PASTA, SUCH AS MACCHERONCINI OR BUCATINI, WILL DO INSTEAD. THE DISH IS ALSO DELICIOUS MADE WITH FRESH ANCHOVIES.

SERVES SIX

INGREDIENTS

2 fennel bulbs, trimmed
a large pinch of saffron threads
12 sardines, backbones and
  heads removed
60ml/4 tbsp olive oil
2 shallots, finely chopped
2 garlic cloves, finely chopped
2 fresh red chillies, seeded and
  finely chopped
4 drained canned anchovy fillets, or
  8–12 pitted black olives, chopped
30ml/2 tbsp capers
75g/3oz/¾ cup pine nuts
450g/1lb pappardelle
butter, for greasing
30ml/2 tbsp grated Pecorino cheese
salt and ground black pepper

1 Preheat the oven to 200°C/400°F/ Gas 6. Cut the fennel bulbs in half and cook them in a pan of lightly salted boiling water with the saffron threads for about 10 minutes, until tender. Drain, reserving the cooking liquid, and cut into small dice. Then finely chop the sardines, season with salt and ground black pepper and set aside until required.

2 Heat the olive oil in a pan, add the shallots and garlic and cook until lightly coloured. Add the chillies and sardines and cook for 3 minutes. Stir in the fennel and cook gently for 3 minutes. If the mixture seems dry, add a little of the reserved fennel water.

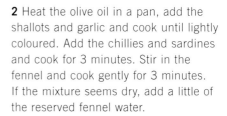

3 Add the anchovies or olives and cook for 1 minute; stir in the capers and pine nuts, and season. Simmer for 3 minutes more, then turn off the heat.

4 Meanwhile, pour the reserved fennel liquid into a pan and top it up with enough water to cook the pasta. Stir in a little salt, bring to the boil and add the pappardelle. Cook dried pasta for about 12 minutes; fresh pasta until it rises to the surface of the water. When the pasta is just tender, drain it.

5 Grease a shallow ovenproof dish and put in a layer of pasta, then make a layer of the sardine mixture. Continue until all the pasta and sardine mixture have been used, finishing with the fish. Sprinkle over the Pecorino; bake for 15 minutes, until bubbling and golden.

LOBSTER RAVIOLI

IT IS ESSENTIAL TO USE HOME-MADE PASTA TO OBTAIN THE DELICACY AND THINNESS THAT THIS SUPERB FILLING DESERVES. BEFORE YOU START THE RECIPE, MAKE A WELL-FLAVOURED FISH STOCK, INCLUDING THE LOBSTER SHELL AND HEAD.

SERVES SIX AS A STARTER,
FOUR AS A MAIN COURSE

INGREDIENTS
1 lobster, about 450g/1lb, cooked
   and taken out of the shell
2 soft white bread slices, about
   50g/2oz, crusts removed
200ml/7fl oz/scant 1 cup fish stock,
   made with the lobster shell
1 egg
250ml/8fl oz/1 cup double
   (heavy) cream
15ml/1 tbsp chopped fresh chives,
   plus extra to garnish
15ml/1 tbsp finely chopped fresh chervil
salt and ground white pepper
fresh chives, to garnish
For the pasta dough
225g/8oz/2 cups strong plain (all-
   purpose) flour
2 eggs, plus 2 egg yolks
For the mushroom sauce
a large pinch of saffron threads
25g/1oz/2 tbsp butter
2 shallots, finely chopped
200g/7oz/3 cups button (white)
   mushrooms, finely chopped
juice of ½ lemon
200ml/7fl oz/scant 1 cup double
   (heavy) cream

1 Make the pasta dough. Sift the flour with a pinch of salt. Put into a food processor with the eggs and extra yolks; process until the mixture resembles coarse breadcrumbs. Turn out on to a floured surface; knead to a smooth dough. Wrap in clear film (plastic wrap) and rest in the refrigerator for 1 hour.

2 Meanwhile, make the lobster filling. Cut the lobster meat into large chunks and place in a bowl. Tear the white bread into small pieces and soak them in 45ml/3 tbsp of the fish stock. Place in a food processor with half the egg and 30–45ml/2–3 tbsp of the double cream and process until smooth. Stir the mixture into the lobster meat, then add the chives and chervil and season to taste with salt and white pepper.

3 Roll the ravioli dough to a thickness of 3mm/⅛in, preferably using a pasta machine. The process can be done by hand with a rolling pin but is quite hard work. Divide the dough into four rectangles and dust each rectangle lightly with flour.

4 Spoon six equal heaps of filling on to one sheet of pasta, leaving about 3cm/1¼in between each pile of filling. Lightly beat the remaining egg with a tablespoon of water and brush it over the pasta between the piles of filling. Cover with a second sheet of pasta. Repeat with the other two sheets of pasta and remaining filling.

5 Using your fingertips, press the top layer of dough down well between the piles of filling, making sure each is well sealed. Cut between the heaps with a 7.5cm/3in fluted pastry cutter or a pasta wheel to make twelve ravioli.

6 Place the ravioli in a single layer on a baking sheet, cover with clear film or a damp cloth, and put in the refrigerator while you make the sauces.

7 Make the mushroom sauce. Soak the saffron in 15ml/1 tbsp warm water. Melt the butter in a pan and cook the shallots over a low heat until they are soft but not coloured.

8 Add the chopped mushrooms and lemon juice and continue to cook over a low heat until almost all the liquid has evaporated. Stir in the saffron, with its soaking water, and the cream, then cook gently, stirring occasionally, until the sauce has thickened. Keep warm while you cook the ravioli.

9 In another pan, bring the remaining fish stock to the boil, stir in the rest of the cream and bubble to make a slightly thickened sauce. Season to taste and keep warm. Bring a large pan of salted water to a rolling boil. Gently drop in the ravioli (left) and cook for 3–4 minutes, until the pasta is just tender.

10 Place two ravioli (three for a main course) on to the centre of individual warmed plates, spoon over a little of the mushroom sauce and pour a ribbon of fish sauce around the edge. Serve immediately, garnished with chopped and whole fresh chives.

LINGUINE <u>ALLE</u> VONGOLE

USE THE SMALLEST CLAMS YOU CAN FIND FOR THIS RECIPE. YOU WILL HAVE GREAT FUN SUCKING THEM OUT OF THEIR SHELLS. IF YOU CAN'T FIND LINGUINE, USE THIN SPAGHETTI.

SERVES FOUR AS A MAIN COURSE,
<u>SIX AS AN APPETIZER</u>

INGREDIENTS
675g/1½lb small clams
45ml/3 tbsp olive oil
2 fat garlic cloves, finely chopped
15ml/1 tbsp anchovy paste, or
  4 drained canned anchovy fillets,
  finely chopped
400g/14oz can chopped tomatoes
30ml/2 tbsp finely chopped fresh
  flat leaf parsley
450g/1lb linguine
salt and ground black pepper

1 Wash and scrub the clams, then put them in a large pan. Cover the pan and place it over a high heat for 3–4 minutes, shaking the pan occasionally, until all the clams have opened. Discard any that remain closed. Strain the clams, reserving the juices. Shell the clams, if you like.

2 Heat the oil in a pan, add the garlic and cook gently for 2 minutes, until lightly coloured. Stir in the anchovy paste or chopped fillets, then the tomatoes and the reserved clam juices. Add the parsley, bring to the boil, then lower the heat and simmer, uncovered, for 20 minutes, until the sauce is well reduced and full of flavour. Season to taste.

3 Cook the linguine in plenty of lightly salted boiling water until just tender. Drain the pasta, then tip it back into the pan. Add the clams to the tomato and anchovy sauce, mix together well then pour the sauce over the linguine and toss until the pasta is well coated. Serve immediately.

BLACK FETTUCCINE <u>WITH</u> SEAFOOD

THE DRAMATIC BLACK PASTA MAKES A WONDERFUL CONTRASTING BACKGROUND FOR THE PINK, WHITE AND GOLDEN SHELLFISH. USE WHATEVER SHELLFISH ARE AVAILABLE; TINY CUTTLEFISH, SMALL SQUID, CLAMS OR RAZORSHELL CLAMS ARE DELICIOUS IN THIS DISH.

SERVES FOUR AS A MAIN COURSE,
<u>SIX AS AN APPETIZER</u>

INGREDIENTS
800g/1¾lb live mussels, scrubbed
  and bearded
45ml/3 tbsp olive oil
105ml/7 tbsp dry white wine
2 fat garlic cloves, chopped
150g/5oz queen scallops
200g/7oz raw prawns (shrimp),
  partially shelled
400g/14oz black fettuccine,
  preferably fresh
salt and ground black pepper
30ml/2 tbsp chopped fresh
  flat leaf parsley, to garnish

COOK'S TIP
If you can't find black pasta, use green spinach tagliatelle or fettuccine instead.

1 Put the mussels in a pan with 15ml/ 1 tbsp of the oil. Add the wine, set over a high heat, cover and steam for about 3 minutes, shaking the pan occasionally, until all the mussels have opened. Discard any shellfish that remain closed. Leave to cool in the pan, then lift out and shell some of the mussels. Strain the cooking liquid and set it aside until required.

2 Heat the remaining oil in a large, deep frying pan. Add the chopped garlic and cook for 1 minute, without letting it brown. Add the queen scallops and cook for about 1–2 minutes, tossing them about until they turn opaque. Add the prawns and cook for 1 minute more, then remove the shellfish with a slotted spoon to a bowl and set it aside. Keep the frying pan handy; it will be needed for the sauce.

3 Meanwhile, cook the pasta in a large pan of lightly salted boiling water according to the packet instructions until just tender; fresh pasta will take only about 2 minutes. Drain.

4 Pour the reserved mussel liquid into the frying pan and bring it to the boil. Lower the heat and season. Return the shellfish to the pan, heat for a few seconds, then stir in the pasta. Toss well, sprinkle the parsley on top and serve.

STIR-FRIED NOODLES IN SHELLFISH SAUCE

THE CHINESE WOULD HAVE US BELIEVE THAT IT WAS THEY WHO INVENTED PASTA, SO IT SEEMS APPROPRIATE TO INCLUDE A CHINESE-STYLE PASTA DISH.

SERVES SIX TO EIGHT AS AN APPETIZER
FOUR AS A MAIN COURSE

INGREDIENTS

225g/8oz Chinese egg noodles
8 spring onions (scallions), trimmed
8 asparagus spears, plus extra
  steamed asparagus spears, to
  serve (optional)
30ml/2 tbsp stir-fry oil
5cm/2in piece fresh root ginger,
  peeled and cut into very fine sticks
3 garlic cloves, chopped
60ml/4 tbsp oyster sauce
450g/1lb cooked crab meat (all
  white, or two-thirds white and
  one-third brown)
30ml/2 tbsp rice wine vinegar
15–30ml/1–2 tbsp light
  soy sauce

1 Put the noodles in a large pan or wok, cover with lightly salted boiling water, place a lid on top and leave for 3–4 minutes, or for the time suggested on the packet. Drain and set aside.

2 Cut off the green spring onion tops and slice them thinly. Set aside. Cut the white parts into 2cm/¾in lengths and quarter them lengthways. Cut the asparagus spears on the diagonal into 2cm/¾in pieces.

3 Heat the stir-fry oil in a pan or wok until very hot, then add the ginger, garlic and white spring onion batons. Stir-fry over a high heat for 1 minute. Add the oyster sauce, crab meat, rice wine vinegar and soy sauce to taste. Stir-fry for about 2 minutes, until the crab and sauce are hot. Add the noodles and toss until heated through. At the last moment, toss in the spring onion tops and serve with a few extra asparagus spears, if you like.

SHELLFISH PAELLA

THERE ARE AS MANY VERSIONS OF PAELLA AS THERE ARE REGIONS OF SPAIN. THOSE FROM NEAR THE COAST CONTAIN A LOT OF SHELLFISH, WHILE INLAND VERSIONS ADD CHICKEN OR PORK. HERE THE ONLY MEAT IS THE CHORIZO, ESSENTIAL FOR AN AUTHENTIC FLAVOUR.

SERVES FOUR

INGREDIENTS

45ml/3 tbsp olive oil
1 Spanish onion, chopped
2 fat garlic cloves, chopped
150g/5oz chorizo sausage, sliced
300g/11oz small squid, cleaned
1 red (bell) pepper, cut into strips
4 tomatoes, peeled, seeded and
 diced, or 200g/7oz can tomatoes
500ml/17fl oz/generous 2 cups
 chicken stock
105ml/7 tbsp dry white wine
200g/7oz/1 cup short grain Spanish
 rice or risotto rice
a large pinch of saffron threads
150g/5oz/1 cup fresh or frozen peas
12 large cooked prawns (shrimp), in
 the shell, or 8 langoustines
450g/1lb fresh mussels, scrubbed
450g/1lb medium clams, scrubbed
salt and ground black pepper

1 Heat the olive oil in a paella pan or wok, add the onion and garlic and cook until translucent. Add the chorizo and cook until lightly golden.

2 If the squid are very small, leave them whole, otherwise cut the bodies into rings and the tentacles into pieces. Add the squid to the pan and sauté over a high heat for 2 minutes.

3 Stir in the pepper strips and tomatoes and simmer gently for 5 minutes, until the pepper strips are tender. Pour in the stock and wine, stir well and bring to the boil.

4 Stir in the rice and saffron threads and season well with salt and pepper. Spread the contents of the pan evenly. Bring the liquid back to the boil, then lower the heat and simmer gently for about 10 minutes.

5 Add the peas, prawns or langoustines, mussels and clams, stirring them gently into the rice.

6 Cook the paella gently for a further 15–20 minutes, until the rice is tender and all the mussels and clams have opened. If any remain closed, discard them. If the paella seems dry, add a little more hot chicken stock. Gently stir everything together and serve piping hot.

RISOTTO NERO

IF YOU HAPPEN TO HAVE SOME SQUID OR CUTTLEFISH COMPLETE WITH INK SACS, RETRIEVE THE INK YOURSELF TO MAKE THIS BLACK RISOTTO. OTHERWISE, YOU CAN BUY SACHETS OF SQUID OR CUTTLEFISH INK AT FISHMONGERS AND SOME DELICATESSENS.

SERVES FOUR

INGREDIENTS
  450g/1lb small cuttlefish or squid,
    with their ink, or 350g/12oz
    cuttlefish and 4 sachets cuttlefish
    or squid ink
  1.2 litres/2 pints/5 cups light
    fish stock
  50g/2oz/¼ cup butter
  30ml/2 tbsp olive oil
  3 shallots, finely chopped
  350g/12oz/1¾ cups risotto rice
  105ml/7 tbsp dry white wine
  30ml/2 tbsp chopped fresh
    flat leaf parsley
  salt and ground black pepper

1 If the cuttlefish or squid contain ink, squeeze it out into a small bowl and set it aside. Cut the bodies into thin rings and chop the tentacles. Set aside.

2 Add the ink to the fish stock. Bring to the boil and lower the heat so that the liquid is at a gentle simmer. Heat half the butter and all the olive oil in a large pan. Add the chopped shallots and cook for about 3 minutes, until they are soft and translucent.

COOK'S TIP
If you prefer, make the risotto without the cuttlefish or squid and serve it with other fish or shellfish.

3 Add the cuttlefish or squid and cook very gently for 5–7 minutes, until tender. Add the rice and stir well to coat all the grains with fat. Pour in the wine and simmer until most of it has been absorbed by the rice. Add a ladleful of the hot stock and cook, stirring constantly, until it has been absorbed.

4 Continue cooking and stirring for 20–25 minutes, adding the remaining stock a ladleful at a time after the previous quantity has been absorbed.

5 Season to taste, then stir in the parsley. Beat in the remaining butter to make the risotto shiny. Spoon the risotto into four warmed dishes and serve.

SHELLFISH RISOTTO

MOST SUPERMARKETS NOW STOCK PACKS OF READY-PREPARED MIXED SHELLFISH, SUCH AS PRAWNS, SQUID AND MUSSELS, WHICH ARE IDEAL FOR MAKING THIS QUICK AND EASY RISOTTO.

SERVES FOUR

INGREDIENTS
 1 litre/1¾ pints/4 cups fish or
  shellfish stock
 50g/2oz/¼ cup butter
 2 shallots, chopped
 2 garlic cloves, chopped
 350g/12oz/1¾ cups risotto rice
 150ml/¼ pint/⅔ cup dry white wine
 2.5ml/½ tsp powdered saffron, or a
  pinch of saffron threads
 400g/14oz mixed prepared shellfish
 30ml/2 tbsp freshly grated
  Parmesan cheese
 30ml/2 tbsp chopped fresh
  flat leaf parsley, to garnish
 salt and ground black pepper

1 Pour the fish or shellfish stock into a large pan. Bring it to the boil, then reduce the heat and keep it at a gentle simmer. The water needs to be hot when it is added to the rice.

2 Melt the butter in a heavy pan, add the shallots and garlic and cook over a low heat until soft but not coloured. Add the rice, stir well to coat the grains with butter, then pour in the wine. Cook over a medium heat, stirring occasionally, until all the wine has been absorbed by the rice.

COOK'S TIP
It is essential to use risotto rice for this dish. You can buy arborio or carnaroli risotto rice in an Italian delicatessen or a large supermarket.

3 Add a ladleful of hot stock and the saffron and cook, stirring constantly, until the liquid has been absorbed. Add the shellfish and stir well. Continue to add stock a ladleful at a time, waiting until each quantity has been absorbed before adding more. Stir the mixture for about 20 minutes, until the rice is swollen and creamy, but still with a little bite in the middle.

VARIATION
Use peeled prawns (shrimp), or cubes of fish, such as cod or salmon, in place of the mixed prepared shellfish.

4 Vigorously mix in the freshly grated Parmesan cheese and season to taste, then sprinkle over the chopped parsley and serve immediately.

LIGHT AND HEALTHY DISHES

What could be healthier than a meal based on simply cooked fish and shellfish?

We should all include fish in our diet at least twice a week, particularly the oily fish

that are so beneficial to health. Here are vibrant, attractive dishes certain to inspire, such as

Roast Cod with Pancetta and Beans, Moroccan Spiced Mackerel, and Hoki

Stir-Fry. All are quick to prepare and so full of fresh, natural flavours that

healthy eating becomes pure pleasure.

STEAMED LETTUCE-WRAPPED SOLE

IF YOU CAN AFFORD IT, USE DOVER SOLE FILLETS FOR THIS RECIPE; IF NOT, LEMON SOLE, TROUT, PLAICE, FLOUNDER AND BRILL ARE ALL EXCELLENT COOKED THIS WAY.

SERVES FOUR

INGREDIENTS

2 large sole fillets, skinned
15ml/1 tbsp sesame seeds
15ml/1 tbsp sunflower or
   groundnut (peanut) oil
10ml/2 tsp sesame oil
2.5cm/1in piece fresh root ginger,
   peeled and grated
3 garlic cloves, finely chopped
15ml/1 tbsp soy sauce or Thai fish
   sauce (*nam pla*)
juice of 1 lemon
2 spring onions (scallions), thinly sliced
8 large soft lettuce leaves
12 large fresh mussels, scrubbed
   and bearded

1 Cut the sole fillets in half lengthways. Season; set aside. Prepare a steamer.

2 Heat a heavy frying pan until hot. Toast the sesame seeds lightly but do not allow them to burn. Set aside in a bowl until required.

3 Heat the oils in the frying pan over a medium heat. Add the ginger and garlic and cook until lightly coloured; stir in the soy sauce or fish sauce, lemon juice and spring onions. Remove from the heat; stir in the toasted sesame seeds.

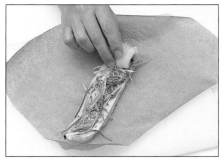

4 Lay the pieces of fish on baking parchment, skinned-side up; spread each evenly with the ginger mixture. Roll up each piece, starting at the tail end. Place on a baking sheet.

5 Plunge the lettuce leaves into the boiling water you have prepared for the steamer and immediately lift them out with tongs or a slotted spoon. Lay them out flat on kitchen paper and gently pat them dry. Wrap each sole parcel in two lettuce leaves, making sure that the filling is well covered to keep it in place.

6 Arrange the fish parcels in a steamer basket, cover and steam over simmering water for 8 minutes. Add the mussels and steam for 2–4 minutes, until opened. Discard any that remain closed. Put the parcels on individual warmed plates, halve and garnish with mussels. Serve immediately.

SMOKED HADDOCK WITH MUSTARD CABBAGE

THIS SIMPLE DISH TAKES LESS THAN TWENTY MINUTES TO MAKE AND IS QUITE DELICIOUS. SERVE IT WITH NEW POTATOES.

2 Meanwhile put the haddock in a large shallow pan with the milk, onion and bay leaves. Add the lemon slices and peppercorns. Bring to simmering point, cover and poach until the fish flakes easily when tested with the tip of a sharp knife. Depending in the thickness of the fish, this takes 8–10 minutes. Remove the pan from the heat and set aside. Preheat the grill (broiler).

3 Cut the tomatoes in half horizontally, season them with salt and pepper and grill (broil) until lightly browned. Drain the cabbage, refresh under cold water and drain again.

4 Melt the butter in a shallow pan or wok, add the cabbage and toss over the heat for 2 minutes. Mix in the mustard and season to taste, then tip the cabbage into a warmed serving dish.

SERVES FOUR

INGREDIENTS

  1 Savoy or pointu cabbage
  675g/1½lb undyed smoked
   haddock fillet
  300ml/½ pint/1¼ cups milk
  ½ onion, peeled and sliced into rings
  2 bay leaves
  ½ lemon, sliced
  4 white peppercorns
  4 ripe tomatoes
  50g/2oz/¼ cup butter
  30ml/2 tbsp wholegrain mustard
  juice of 1 lemon
  salt and ground black pepper
  30ml/2 tbsp chopped fresh parsley,
   to garnish

1 Cut the cabbage in half, remove the central core and thick ribs, then shred the cabbage. Cook in a pan of lightly salted boiling water, or steam over boiling water for about 10 minutes, until just tender. Leave in the pan or steamer until required.

5 Drain the haddock. Skin and cut the fish into four pieces. Place on top of the cabbage with some onion rings and grilled tomato halves. Pour on the lemon juice, then sprinkle with chopped parsley and serve.

BAKED SEA BASS WITH FENNEL

SEA BASS HAS A WONDERFUL FLAVOUR, BUT CHEAPER ALTERNATIVES, SUCH AS SNAPPER, BREAM OR PORGY, CAN BE USED. SERVE WITH CRISPLY COOKED GREEN BEANS TOSSED IN OLIVE OIL AND GARLIC.

SERVES FOUR

INGREDIENTS
4 fennel bulbs, trimmed
4 tomatoes, peeled and diced
8 drained canned anchovy fillets,
  halved lengthways
a large pinch of saffron threads,
  soaked in 30ml/2 tbsp hot water
150ml/¼ pint/⅔ cup chicken or
  fish stock
2 red or yellow (bell) peppers, seeded
  and each cut into 12 strips
4 garlic cloves, chopped
15ml/1 tbsp chopped fresh marjoram
45ml/3 tbsp olive oil
1 sea bass, about 1.75kg/4–4½lb,
  scaled and cleaned
salt and ground black pepper
chopped parsley, to garnish

1 Preheat the oven to 200°C/400°F/ Gas 6. Quarter the fennel bulbs lengthways. Cook in lightly salted boiling water for 5 minutes, until barely tender. Drain and arrange in a shallow ovenproof dish. Season with pepper; set aside.

2 Spoon the diced tomatoes and anchovy strips on top of the fennel. Stir the saffron and its soaking water into the stock and pour the mixture over the tomatoes. Lay the strips of pepper alongside the fennel and sprinkle with the garlic and marjoram. Drizzle 30ml/ 2 tbsp of the olive oil over the peppers and season with salt and pepper.

VARIATION
If you like, use large pieces of thick-cut halibut or turbot for this dish.

3 Bake the vegetables for 15 minutes. Season the prepared sea bass inside and out and lay it on top of the fennel and pepper mixture. Drizzle the remaining olive oil over the fish and bake for 30–40 minutes more, until the sea bass flesh comes away easily from the bone when tested with the point of a sharp knife. Serve, garnished with parsley.

MOROCCAN SPICED MACKEREL

MACKEREL IS EXTREMELY GOOD FOR YOU, BUT SOME PEOPLE FIND ITS HEALTHY OILINESS TOO MUCH TO TAKE. THE MOROCCAN SPICES IN THIS RECIPE COUNTERACT THE RICHNESS OF THE FISH.

SERVES FOUR

INGREDIENTS
150ml/¼ pint/⅔ cup sunflower oil
15ml/1 tbsp paprika
5–10ml/1–2 tsp harissa (chilli sauce)
  or chilli powder
10ml/2 tsp ground cumin
10ml/2 tsp ground coriander
2 garlic cloves, crushed
juice of 2 lemons
30ml/2 tbsp chopped fresh
  mint leaves
30ml/2 tbsp chopped fresh
  coriander (cilantro)
4 mackerel, cleaned
salt and ground black pepper
mint sprigs, to garnish
lemon wedges, to serve

1 In a bowl, whisk together the oil, spices, garlic and lemon juice. Season, then stir in the mint and coriander.

2 Make two or three diagonal slashes on either side of each mackerel so that they may absorb the marinade. Pour the marinade into a shallow non-metallic dish that is large enough to hold the fish in a single layer.

3 Put in the mackerel and turn them over in the marinade, spooning it into the slashes. Cover the dish with clear film (plastic wrap) and place in the refrigerator for at least 3 hours.

4 When you are ready to cook the mackerel, preheat the grill (broiler) to medium-high. Transfer the fish to the grill rack and grill (broil) for 5–7 minutes on each side until just cooked, turning the fish once and basting them several times with the marinade. Serve hot or cold with lemon wedges, garnished with mint. Herb-flavoured couscous or rice make good accompaniments.

COOK'S TIP
These spicy mackerel can be cooked on a barbecue. Make sure the coals are very hot before you begin cooking. Arrange the fish on a large hinged rack to make turning easier and barbecue (grill) for 5–7 minutes, turning once.

VARIATION
Trout, bonito, trevally or bluefish are also good cooked this way.

ASIAN FISH EN PAPILLOTE

THE AROMATIC SMELL THAT WAFTS OUT OF THESE FISH PARCELS AS YOU OPEN THEM IS DELICIOUSLY TEMPTING. IF YOU DON'T LIKE ASIAN FLAVOURS, USE WHITE WINE, HERBS AND THINLY SLICED VEGETABLES, OR MEDITERRANEAN INGREDIENTS, SUCH AS TOMATOES, BASIL AND OLIVES.

SERVES FOUR

INGREDIENTS

2 carrots
2 courgettes (zucchini)
6 spring onions (scallions)
2.5cm/1in piece fresh root
  ginger, peeled
1 lime
2 garlic cloves, thinly sliced
30ml/2 tbsp teriyaki marinade or
  Thai fish sauce (*nam pla*)
5–10ml/1–2 tsp clear sesame oil
4 salmon fillets, about
  200g/7oz each
ground black pepper
rice, to serve

VARIATION
Thick fillets of hake, halibut, hoki and fresh or undyed smoked haddock and cod can all be used for this dish.

1 Cut the carrots, courgettes and spring onions into thin sticks and set them aside. Cut the ginger into thin sticks and put these in a small bowl. Using a zester, pare the lime thinly. Add the pared rind to the ginger, with the garlic. Squeeze the lime juice.

2 Place the teriyaki marinade or fish sauce in a bowl and stir in the lime juice and sesame oil.

3 Preheat the oven to 220ºC/425ºF/ Gas 7. Cut out four rounds of baking parchment, each with a diameter of 40cm/16in. Season the salmon with pepper. Lay a fillet on one side of each paper round, about 3cm/1¼in off centre. Sprinkle a quarter of the ginger mixture over each and pile a quarter of the vegetable sticks on top. Spoon a quarter of the teriyaki or fish sauce mixture over the top.

4 Fold the bare side of the baking parchment over the salmon and roll the edges of the parchment over to seal each parcel very tightly.

5 Place the salmon parcels on a baking sheet and cook in the oven for about 10–12 minutes, depending on the thickness of the fillets. Put the parcels on plates and serve with rice.

ROAST COD <u>WITH</u> PANCETTA <u>AND</u> BEANS

THICK COD STEAKS WRAPPED IN PANCETTA AND ROASTED MAKE A SUPERB SUPPER DISH WHEN SERVED ON A BED OF BUTTER BEANS, WITH SWEET AND JUICY CHERRY TOMATOES ON THE SIDE.

SERVES FOUR

INGREDIENTS

    200g/7oz/1 cup butter (lima) beans,
      soaked overnight in cold water
    2 leeks, thinly sliced
    2 garlic cloves, chopped
    8 fresh sage leaves
    90ml/6 tbsp fruity olive oil
    8 thin slices of pancetta
    4 thick cod steaks, skinned
    12 cherry tomatoes
    salt and ground black pepper

1 Drain the beans, tip into a pan and cover with cold water. Bring to the boil and skim off the foam on the surface. Lower the heat, then stir in the leeks, garlic, 4 sage leaves and 30ml/2 tbsp of the olive oil. Simmer for 1–1½ hours until the beans are tender, adding more water if necessary. Drain, return to the pan, season, stir in 30ml/2 tbsp olive oil and keep warm.

2 Preheat the oven to 200°C/400°F/ Gas 6. Wrap two slices of pancetta around the edge of each cod steak, tying it on with kitchen string or securing it with a wooden cocktail stick or toothpick. Insert a sage leaf between the pancetta and the cod. Season the fish.

VARIATION
You can use cannellini beans for this recipe, and streaky (fatty) bacon instead of pancetta. It is also good made with halibut, hake, haddock or salmon.

3 Heat a heavy frying pan, add 15ml/ 1 tbsp of the remaining oil and seal the cod steaks, two at a time, for 1 minute on each side. Transfer them to an ovenproof dish and roast in the oven for 5 minutes.

4 Add the tomatoes to the dish and drizzle over the remaining olive oil. Roast for 5 minutes more, until the cod steaks are cooked but still juicy. Serve them on a bed of butter beans with the roasted tomatoes. Garnish with parsley.

HERBED CHARGRILLED SHARK STEAKS

SHARK IS VERY LOW IN FAT, WITH DENSE, WELL-FLAVOURED FLESH. OTHER CLOSE-TEXTURED FISH LIKE TUNA, BONITO AND MARLIN WORK EQUALLY WELL IN THIS RECIPE, WHICH IS IDEAL FOR A BARBECUE. SERVE THE FISH WITH A TANGY TOMATO SALAD.

SERVES FOUR

INGREDIENTS

45ml/3 tbsp olive oil
2 fresh bay leaves, chopped
15ml/1 tbsp chopped fresh basil
15ml/1 tbsp chopped fresh oregano
30ml/2 tbsp chopped fresh parsley
5ml/1 tsp finely chopped
   fresh rosemary
5ml/1 tsp fresh thyme leaves
2 garlic cloves, crushed
4 pieces drained sun-dried tomatoes
   in oil, chopped
4 shark steaks, about 200g/7oz each
juice of 1 lemon
15ml/1 tbsp drained small
   capers in vinegar (optional)
salt and ground black pepper

1 Whisk the oil, herbs, garlic and sun-dried tomatoes in a bowl, then pour the mixture into a shallow dish that is large enough to hold the shark steaks in a single layer. Season the shark steaks with salt and pepper and brush the lemon juice over both sides. Lay the fish in the dish, turning the steaks to coat them all over. Cover and marinate in the refrigerator for 1–2 hours.

2 Heat a ridged griddle pan or barbecue until it is very hot. Lift the shark steaks out of the marinade, pat dry with kitchen paper and grill (broil) or cook on the barbecue for about 5 minutes on each side, until they are cooked through. Pour the marinade into a small pan and bring to the boil. Stir in the capers, if using. Spoon over the shark steaks and serve immediately.

CHINESE-STYLE SCALLOPS AND PRAWNS

SERVE THIS LIGHT, DELICATE DISH FOR LUNCH OR SUPPER ACCOMPANIED BY AROMATIC STEAMED RICE OR FINE RICE NOODLES AND STIR-FRIED PAK CHOI.

SERVES FOUR

INGREDIENTS

15ml/1 tbsp stir-fry or sunflower oil
500g/1¼lb raw tiger prawns (jumbo
   shrimp), peeled
1 star anise
225g/8oz scallops, halved if large
2.5cm/1in piece fresh root ginger,
   peeled and grated
2 garlic cloves, thinly sliced
1 red (bell) pepper, seeded and cut
   into thin strips
115g/4oz/1¾ cups shiitake or button
   (white) mushrooms, thinly sliced
juice of 1 lemon
5ml/1 tsp cornflour (cornstarch),
   mixed with 30ml/2 tbsp cold water
30ml/2 tbsp light soy sauce
chopped fresh chives, to garnish
salt and ground black pepper

1 Heat the oil in a wok until very hot. Put in the prawns and star anise and stir-fry over a high heat for 2 minutes. Add the scallops, ginger and garlic and stir-fry for 1 minute more, by which time the prawns should have turned pink and the scallops opaque. Season with a little salt and plenty of pepper and then remove from the wok using a slotted spoon. Discard the star anise.

2 Add the red pepper and mushrooms to the wok and stir-fry for 1–2 minutes. Pour in the lemon juice, cornflour paste and soy sauce, bring to the boil and bubble for 1–2 minutes, stirring constantly, until the sauce is smooth and slightly thickened.

3 Stir the prawns and scallops into the sauce, cook for a few seconds until heated through, then season with salt and ground black pepper and serve garnished with chopped chives.

VARIATIONS
Use other prepared shellfish in this dish; try thinly sliced rings of squid, or mussels or clams, or substitute chunks of firm white fish, such as monkfish fillet, for the scallops.

FILO FISH PIES

THESE LIGHT FILO-WRAPPED FISH PIES CAN BE MADE WITH ANY FIRM WHITE FISH FILLETS, SUCH AS ORANGE ROUGHY, COD, HALIBUT OR HOKI. SERVE WITH SALAD LEAVES AND MAYONNAISE ON THE SIDE.

2 Brush the inside of six 13cm/5in tartlet tins (muffin pans) with a little of the melted butter. Fit a piece of filo pastry into the tins, draping it so that it hangs over the sides. Brush with butter, then add another sheet at right-angles to the first. Brush with butter. Continue to line the tins in this way.

3 Spread the spinach evenly over the pastry. Add the diced fish and season well. Stir the chives into the crème fraîche and spread the mixture over the top of the fish. Sprinkle the dill over.

4 Draw the overhanging pieces of pastry together and scrunch lightly to make a lid. Brush with butter. Bake for about 15–20 minutes, until golden brown.

SERVES SIX

INGREDIENTS
  400g/14oz spinach, trimmed
  1 egg, lightly beaten
  2 garlic cloves, crushed
  450g/1lb orange roughy or other
    white fish fillet
  juice of 1 lemon
  50g/2oz/¼ cup butter, melted
  8–12 filo pastry sheets, thawed
    if frozen, quartered
  15ml/1 tbsp finely chopped
    fresh chives
  200ml/7fl oz/scant 1 cup half-fat
    crème fraîche
  15ml/1 tbsp chopped fresh dill
  salt and ground black pepper

VARIATION
To make one large pie, use a 20cm/8in tin (pan) and cook for 45 minutes.

1 Preheat the oven to 190°C/375°F/ Gas 5. Wash the spinach, then cook it in a lidded heavy pan with just the water that clings to the leaves. As soon as the leaves are tender, drain, squeeze as dry as possible and chop. Put the spinach in a bowl, add the egg and garlic, season with salt and pepper and set aside. Dice the fish and place it in a bowl. Stir in the lemon juice. Season with salt and pepper and toss lightly.

HOKI STIR-FRY

ANY FIRM WHITE FISH, SUCH AS MONKFISH, HAKE OR COD, CAN BE USED FOR THIS ATTRACTIVE STIR-FRY. VARY THE VEGETABLES ACCORDING TO WHAT IS AVAILABLE, BUT TRY TO INCLUDE AT LEAST THREE DIFFERENT COLOURS. SHRIMP-FRIED RICE WOULD BE THE PERFECT ACCOMPANIMENT.

SERVES FOUR TO SIX

INGREDIENTS

675g/1½lb hoki fillet, skinned
pinch of five-spice powder
2 carrots
115g/4oz/1 cup mangetouts (snow peas)
115g/4oz asparagus spears
4 spring onions (scallions)
45ml/3 tbsp groundnut (peanut) oil
2.5cm/1in piece fresh root ginger,
   peeled and cut into thin slivers
2 garlic cloves, finely chopped
300g/11oz beansprouts
8–12 small baby corn cobs
15–30ml/1–2 tbsp light soy sauce
salt and ground black pepper

1 Cut the hoki into finger-size strips and season with salt, pepper and five-spice powder. Cut the carrots diagonally into slices as thin as the mangetouts.

2 Trim the mangetouts. Trim the asparagus spears and cut in half crossways. Trim the spring onions and cut them diagonally into 2cm/¾in pieces, keeping the white and green parts separate. Set aside.

3 Heat a wok, then pour in the oil. As soon as it is hot, add the ginger and garlic. Stir-fry for 1 minute, then add the white parts of the spring onions and cook for 1 minute more.

COOK'S TIP
When adding the oil to the hot wok, drizzle it around the inner rim like a necklace. The oil will run down to coat the entire surface of the wok. Swirl the wok to make sure the coating is even.

4 Add the hoki strips and stir-fry for 2–3 minutes, until all the pieces of fish are opaque. Add the beansprouts. Toss them around to coat them in the oil, then put in the carrots, mangetouts, asparagus and corn. Continue to stir-fry for 3–4 minutes, by which time the fish should be cooked, but all the vegetables will still be crunchy. Add soy sauce to taste, toss everything quickly together, then stir in the green parts of the spring onions. Serve immediately.

BRAISED BREAM WITH SHELLFISH

THIS VERSATILE DISH IS EXTREMELY LOW IN CALORIES, BUT FULL OF FLAVOUR. USE ANY MIXTURE OF FRESH OR FROZEN SHELLFISH YOU LIKE (A FEW MUSSELS OR CLAMS IN THE SHELL ARE PARTICULARLY ATTRACTIVE). SERVE WITH NOODLES OR PASTA SHELLS.

SERVES FOUR

INGREDIENTS
30ml/2 tbsp olive oil
1 onion, thinly sliced
1 yellow or orange (bell) pepper,
   seeded and cut into strips
400ml/14fl oz/1⅔ cups well-reduced
   tomato sauce
45ml/3 tbsp dry white wine or
   fish stock
2 courgettes (zucchini), sliced
350g/12oz bream or porgy fillets,
   skinned and cut into 5cm/
   2in chunks
450g/1lb ready-prepared mixed
   shellfish, thawed if frozen
juice of ½ lemon
15ml/1 tbsp shredded fresh marjoram
   or basil leaves
salt and ground black pepper
basil leaves, to garnish
cooked pasta or noodles, to serve

1 Heat the olive oil in a large frying pan. Add the onion slices and yellow or orange pepper strips and stir-fry the vegetables for about 2 minutes, until the onion is translucent.

COOK'S TIP
If you are short of time, use a 400ml/ 14fl oz jar of good quality ready-prepared tomato sauce.

2 Stir in the tomato sauce, with the white wine or fish stock and bring to the boil. Lower the heat, then simmer for about 2 minutes.

3 Add the courgettes and the chunks of fish; cover and cook gently for about 5 minutes, stirring once or twice during this time. Add the shellfish and stir well to coat it with the sauce.

4 Season to taste with salt, pepper and lemon juice, cover the pan and simmer for 2–3 minutes, until heated through. Stir in the shredded marjoram or basil, and garnish with basil leaves. Serve with noodles or pasta.

VARIATIONS
Fillets of snapper, bass or red mullet could be used in place of the bream in this recipe.

MALAYSIAN STEAMED TROUT FILLETS

THIS SIMPLE DISH CAN BE PREPARED EXTREMELY QUICKLY, AND IS SUITABLE FOR ANY FISH FILLETS. SERVE IT ON A BED OF NOODLES ACCOMPANIED BY RIBBONS OF COLOURFUL VEGETABLES.

SERVES FOUR

INGREDIENTS
8 pink trout fillets of even thickness,
   about 115g/4oz each, skinned
45ml/3 tbsp grated creamed coconut
   (coconut cream)
grated rind and juice of 2 limes
45ml/3 tbsp chopped fresh
   coriander (cilantro)
15ml/1 tbsp sunflower oil
2.5–5ml/½–1 tsp chilli oil
salt and ground black pepper
lime slices and coriander (cilantro)
   sprigs, to garnish

1 Cut four rectangles of baking parchment, twice the size of the trout. Place a fillet on each piece and season.

2 Mix together the coconut, lime rind and chopped coriander and spread a quarter of the mixture over each trout fillet. Sandwich another trout fillet on top. Mix the lime juice with the oils, adjusting the quantity of chilli oil to your own taste, and drizzle the mixture over the trout "sandwiches".

3 Prepare a steamer. Fold up the edges of the parchment and pleat them over the trout to make parcels, making sure they are well sealed. Place in the steamer insert and steam over the simmering water for about 10–15 minutes, depending on the thickness of the fish. Serve immediately.

ELEGANT DISHES FOR ENTERTAINING

For sheer elegance, fish and shellfish are hard to beat and so quick to prepare that they make light work of entertaining. A whole fish baked in a salt crust looks intriguing and tastes superb. For breathtaking elegance and taste, treat your guests to Lobster Thermidor, Vegetable-stuffed Squid or Fillets of Turbot with Oysters. Whatever the occasion, delight your guests with these superb party dishes.

HAKE AU POIVRE WITH RED PEPPER RELISH

THIS PISCINE VERSION OF THE CLASSIC STEAK AU POIVRE CAN BE MADE WITH MONKFISH OR COD INSTEAD OF HAKE. VARY THE QUANTITY OF PEPPERCORNS ACCORDING TO YOUR PERSONAL TASTE.

SERVES FOUR

INGREDIENTS
   30–45ml/2–3 tbsp mixed peppercorns
      (black, white, pink and green)
   4 hake steaks, about 175g/6oz each
   30ml/2 tbsp olive oil
For the red (bell) pepper relish
   2 red (bell) peppers
   15ml/1 tbsp olive oil
   2 garlic cloves, chopped
   4 ripe tomatoes, peeled, seeded
      and quartered
   4 drained canned anchovy
      fillets, chopped
   5ml/1 tsp capers
   15ml/1 tbsp balsamic vinegar
   12 fresh basil leaves, shredded, plus
      a few extra to garnish
   salt and ground black pepper

1 Put the peppercorns in a mortar and crush them coarsely with a pestle. Alternatively, put them in a plastic bag and crush them with a rolling pin. Season the hake fillets lightly with salt, then coat them evenly on both sides with the crushed peppercorns. Set the coated fish steaks aside while you make the red pepper relish.

2 Make the relish. Cut the red peppers in half lengthways, remove the core and seeds from each and cut the flesh into 1cm/½in wide strips. Heat the olive oil in a wok or a shallow pan that has a lid. Add the peppers and stir them for about 5 minutes, until they are slightly softened. Stir in the chopped garlic, tomatoes and the anchovies, then cover the pan and simmer the mixture very gently for about 20 minutes, until the peppers are very soft.

3 Tip the contents of the pan into a food processor and process to a coarse purée. Transfer to a bowl and season to taste. Stir in the capers, balsamic vinegar and basil. Keep the relish hot.

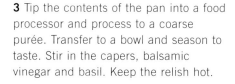

4 Heat the olive oil in a shallow pan, add the hake steaks and cook them, in batches if necessary, for 5 minutes on each side, turning them once or twice, until they are just cooked through.

5 Place the fish on individual plates and spoon a little red pepper relish on to each plate. Garnish with basil leaves and a little extra balsamic vinegar. Serve the rest of the relish separately.

JOHN DORY WITH LIGHT CURRY SAUCE

THIS EXCELLENT COMBINATION OF FLAVOURS ALSO WORKS WELL WITH OTHER FLAT FISH LIKE TURBOT, HALIBUT AND BRILL, OR MORE EXOTIC SPECIES LIKE MAHI-MAHI OR ORANGE ROUGHY. THE CURRY TASTE SHOULD BE VERY SUBTLE, SO USE A MILD CURRY POWDER. SERVE THE FISH WITH PILAU RICE AND MANGO CHUTNEY. IT LOOKS WONDERFUL ARRANGED ON BANANA LEAVES, IF YOU CAN FIND SOME.

SERVES FOUR

INGREDIENTS

    4 John Dory fillets, each about
      175g/6oz, skinned
    15ml/1 tbsp sunflower oil
    25g/1oz/2 tbsp butter
    salt and ground black pepper
    15ml/1 tbsp fresh coriander (cilantro)
      leaves, 4 banana leaves (optional),
      and 1 small mango, peeled and
      diced,to garnish
For the curry sauce
    30ml/2 tbsp sunflower oil
    1 carrot, chopped
    1 onion, chopped
    1 celery stick, chopped
    white of 1 leek, chopped
    2 garlic cloves, crushed
    50g/2oz creamed coconut (coconut
      cream), crumbled
    2 tomatoes, peeled, seeded and diced
    2.5cm/1in piece fresh root
      ginger, grated
    15ml/1 tbsp tomato purée (paste)
    5–10ml/1–2 tsp mild curry powder
    500ml/17fl oz/generous 2 cups
      chicken or fish stock

1 Make the sauce. Heat the oil in a pan; add the vegetables and garlic. Cook gently until soft but not brown.

COOK'S TIP
The coconut sauce must be cooked over a very low heat, so use a heat diffuser if you have one.

2 Add the coconut, tomatoes and ginger. Cook for 1–2 minutes; stir in the tomato purée and curry powder to taste. Add the stock, stir and season.

3 Bring to the boil, then lower the heat, cover the pan and cook the sauce over the lowest heat for about 50 minutes. Stir once or twice to prevent burning. Leave the sauce to cool; pour into a food processor or blender and process until smooth. Return to a clean pan and reheat very gently, adding a little water if too thick.

4 Season the fish fillets with salt and pepper. Heat the oil in a large frying pan, add the butter and heat until sizzling. Put in the fish and cook for about 2–3 minutes on each side, until pale golden and cooked through. Drain on kitchen paper.

5 If you have banana leaves, place these on individual warmed plates and arrange the fillets on top. Pour the sauce around the fish and sprinkle on the finely diced mango. Decorate with coriander leaves and serve immediately.

GRILLED SQUID WITH CHORIZO

THE BEST WAY TO COOK THIS DISH IS ON A GRIDDLE OR IN A RIDGED GRIDDLE PAN. IF YOU HAVE NEITHER, USE AN OVERHEAD GRILL, MAKING SURE IT IS VERY HOT. IF YOU CAN ONLY FIND MEDIUM-SIZE SQUID, ALLOW TWO PER SERVING AND HALVE THEM LENGTHWAYS FROM THE TAIL END TO THE CAVITY.

SERVES SIX

INGREDIENTS
    24 small squid, cleaned
    150ml/¼ pint/⅔ cup extra
      virgin olive oil
    300g/11oz cooking chorizo, cut into
      12 slices
    3 tomatoes, halved and seasoned
      with salt and pepper
    juice of 1 lemon
    24 cooked new potatoes, halved
    fresh rocket (arugula) leaves
    salt and ground black pepper
    lemon slices, to garnish

1 Separate the body and tentacles of the squid and cut the bodies in half lengthways if they are large.

2 Pour half the oil into a bowl, season with salt and pepper, then toss all the squid in the oil. Heat a ridged griddle pan or grill (broiler) to very hot.

3 Grill (broil) the prepared squid bodies for about 45 seconds on each side until the flesh is opaque and tender. Then transfer to a plate and keep hot. Grill the tentacles for about 1 minute on each side, then place them on the plate. Grill the chorizo slices for about 30 seconds on each side, until golden brown, then set them aside with the squid. Grill the tomato halves for 1–2 minutes on each side, until they are softened and browned.

4 Place the potatoes and a handful of rocket in a large bowl.

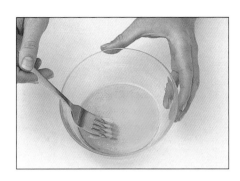

5 Pour the lemon juice into a bowl and whisk in the remaining oil. Season. Reserve 30ml/2 tbsp of this dressing. Pour the dressing over the potatoes and rocket, toss lightly and divide among 6 plates. Pile a portion of the squid, tomatoes and chorizo on each salad, and drizzle over the reserved dressing. Garnish with lemon slices and serve immediately.

SOLE WITH WILD MUSHROOMS

IF POSSIBLE, USE CHANTERELLES FOR THIS DISH; THEIR GLOWING ORANGE COLOUR COMBINES REALLY WONDERFULLY WITH THE INTENSELY GOLDEN SAUCE. OTHERWISE, USE ANY PALE-COLOURED OR OYSTER MUSHROOMS THAT YOU CAN FIND INSTEAD.

SERVES FOUR

INGREDIENTS
    4 Dover sole fillets, about 115g/4oz
      each, skinned
    50g/2oz/4 tbsp butter
    500ml/17fl oz/generous 2 cups
      fish stock
    150g/5oz/2 cups chanterelles
    a large pinch of saffron threads
    150ml/¼ pint/⅔ cup double
      (heavy) cream
    1 egg yolk
    salt and ground white pepper
    finely chopped fresh parsley, and
      parsley sprigs to garnish
    boiled new potatoes, to serve

1 Preheat the oven to 200°C/400°F/ Gas 6. Cut the sole fillets in half lengthways and place them on a board with the skinned side uppermost. Season them with salt and white pepper, then roll them up. Use a little of the butter to grease an ovenproof dish just large enough to hold all the sole fillets in a single layer. Arrange the sole rolls in the dish, then pour over the fish stock. Cover tightly with foil and bake for 12–15 minutes, until cooked through.

2 Meanwhile, pick off any bits of fern or twig from the chanterelles and wipe the mushrooms with a damp cloth. Halve or quarter any large ones. Heat the remaining butter in a frying pan until foaming and sauté the mushrooms for 3–4 minutes, until just tender. Season with salt and pepper and keep hot.

3 Lift the cooked sole fillets out of the cooking liquid and place them on a heated serving dish. Keep hot. Strain the liquid into a small pan, add the saffron threads, set over a very high heat and boil until reduced to about 250ml/8fl oz/1 cup. Stir in the cream and then let the sauce bubble gently once or twice.

4 Lightly beat the egg yolk in a small bowl, pour on a little of the hot sauce and stir well. Stir the mixture into the remaining sauce in the pan and cook over a very low heat for 1–2 minutes, until slightly thickened. Season to taste. Stir the chanterelles into the sauce and pour it over the sole fillets. Garnish with fresh parsley sprigs and serve immediately. Boiled new potatoes make the perfect accompaniment.

LOBSTER THERMIDOR

ONE OF THE CLASSIC FRENCH DISHES, LOBSTER THERMIDOR MAKES A LITTLE LOBSTER GO A LONG WAY. IT IS BEST TO USE ONE BIG RATHER THAN TWO SMALL LOBSTERS, AS A LARGER LOBSTER WILL CONTAIN A HIGHER PROPORTION OF FLESH AND THE MEAT WILL BE SWEETER. IDEALLY, USE A LIVE CRUSTACEAN AND COOK IT YOURSELF, BUT A BOILED LOBSTER FROM THE FISHMONGER WILL DO.

SERVES TWO

INGREDIENTS

  1 large lobster, about
    800g–1kg/1¾–2¼lb, boiled
  45ml/3 tbsp brandy
  25g/1oz/2 tbsp butter
  2 shallots, finely chopped
  115g/4oz/1½ cups button (white)
    mushrooms, thinly sliced
  15ml/1 tbsp plain (all-purpose) flour
  105ml/7 tbsp fish or shellfish stock
  120ml/4fl oz/½ cup double
    (heavy) cream
  5ml/1 tsp Dijon mustard
  2 egg yolks, beaten
  45ml/3 tbsp dry white wine
  45ml/3 tbsp freshly grated Parmesan
  salt, ground black pepper and
    cayenne pepper

1 Split the lobster in half lengthways; crack the claws. Discard the stomach sac; keep the coral for another dish. Keeping each half-shell intact, extract the meat from the tail and claws, then cut into large dice. Place in a shallow dish; sprinkle over the brandy. Cover and set aside. Wipe and dry the half-shells and set them aside.

2 Melt the butter in a pan and cook the shallots over a low heat until soft. Add the mushrooms and cook until just tender, stirring constantly. Stir in the flour and a pinch of cayenne; cook, stirring, for 2 minutes. Gradually add the stock, stirring until the sauce boils and thickens.

3 Stir in the cream and mustard and continue to cook until the sauce is smooth and thick. Season to taste with salt, black pepper and cayenne. Pour half the sauce on to the egg yolks, stir well and return the mixture to the pan. Stir in the wine; adjust the seasoning, being generous with the cayenne.

4 Preheat the grill (broiler) to medium-high. Stir the diced lobster and the brandy into the sauce. Arrange the lobster half-shells in a grill pan and divide the mixture among them. Sprinkle with Parmesan and place under the grill until browned. Serve with steamed rice and mixed salad leaves.

RED MULLET SALTIMBOCCA

THE RICH RED COLOUR OF THE MULLET IS INTENSIFIED BY RUBBING SAFFRON INTO THE SKIN, COMPLEMENTING THE PROSCIUTTO BEAUTIFULLY. SERVE WITH BRIGHTLY COLOURED ROASTED MEDITERRANEAN VEGETABLES AND CRISPLY COOKED GREEN BEANS, IF YOU LIKE.

SERVES FOUR

INGREDIENTS
  8 red mullet or red snapper fillets,
    scaled but not skinned
  a pinch of saffron threads or
    powdered saffron
  15ml/1 tbsp olive oil
  8 fresh sage leaves
  8 thin slices of prosciutto
  25g/1oz/2 tbsp butter
  115g/4oz/1 cup mixed olives
  salt and ground black pepper
For the dressing
  15ml/1 tbsp caster (superfine) sugar
  105ml/7 tbsp balsamic vinegar
  300ml/½ pint/1¼ cups extra virgin
    olive oil
  5cm/2in slice red (bell) pepper, diced
  1 small courgette (zucchini), diced
  1 ripe tomato, peeled, seeded and
    very finely diced

1 Score the fish skin lightly in three or four places. Season both sides of each fillet with salt and ground black pepper. If you are using saffron threads, crumble them over the skin side of each fish fillet, or sprinkle the powdered saffron over the skin. Drizzle on a little olive oil and then rub the saffron in well with your fingertips. This will dramatically enhance the colour of the fish skin .

2 Heat a non-stick frying pan until very hot, then put in the fillets, skin side down, and cook over a high heat for 2 minutes. Turn the fillets over and cook them for 2 minutes more. Drain on kitchen paper and leave until cool enough to handle.

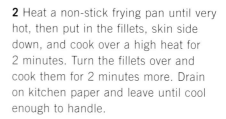

3 Place a sage leaf on each cooked fillet, then wrap the fillets in a slice of prosciutto to cover them completely. Melt the butter in the frying pan and continue to heat until it foams. Fry the ham and red mullet parcels over a high heat for 1–2 minutes on each side, until the ham is pale golden. Transfer to warmed serving plates and keep hot while you make the dressing.

4 Mix the sugar and balsamic vinegar in a small pan, set over a high heat and boil until syrupy.

5 Meanwhile, pour the olive oil into a bowl, stir in the diced vegetables and season. Stir the vinegar syrup into the dressing. Drizzle it over and around the ham-wrapped fish. Place the olives on the plates and serve immediately.

ROAST MONKFISH WITH GARLIC

MONKFISH TIED UP AND COOKED IN THIS WAY IS KNOWN IN FRENCH AS A "GIGOT", BECAUSE IT RESEMBLES A LEG OF LAMB. THE COMBINATION OF MONKFISH AND GARLIC IS SUPERB. FOR A CONTRAST IN COLOUR, SERVE IT WITH VIBRANT GREEN BEANS.

SERVES FOUR TO SIX

INGREDIENTS
    1kg/2¼lb monkfish tail, skinned
    14 fat garlic cloves
    5ml/1 tsp fresh thyme leaves
    30ml/2 tbsp olive oil
    juice of 1 lemon
    2 bay leaves
    salt and ground black pepper

1 Preheat the oven to 220°C/425°F/ Gas 7. Remove any membrane from the monkfish tail and cut out the central bone. Peel 2 garlic cloves and cut them into thin slivers. Sprinkle a quarter of these and half the thyme leaves over the cut side of the fish, then close it up and use fine kitchen string to tie it into a neat shape, like a boned piece of meat. Pat dry with kitchen paper.

2 Make incisions on either side of the fish and push in the remaining garlic slivers. Heat half the olive oil in a frying pan which can safely be used in the oven. When the oil is hot, put in the monkfish and brown it all over for about 5 minutes, until evenly coloured. Season with salt and pepper, sprinkle with lemon juice and sprinkle over the remaining thyme.

3 Tuck the bay leaves under the monkfish, arrange the remaining (unpeeled) garlic cloves around it and drizzle the remaining olive oil over the fish and the garlic. Transfer the frying pan to the oven and roast the monkfish for 20–25 minutes, until the flesh is cooked through.

4 Place on a warmed serving dish with the garlic and some green beans. To serve, remove the string and cut the monkfish into 2cm/¾in thick slices.

COOK'S TIPS
• The garlic heads can be used whole.
• When serving the monkfish, invite each guest to pop out the soft garlic pulp with a fork and spread it over the monkfish.
• Use two smaller monkfish tails.

SEA BASS WITH GINGER AND LEEKS

YOU CAN USE WHOLE FISH OR THICK FILLETS FOR THIS RECIPE, WHICH IS ALSO EXCELLENT MADE WITH BREAM, PORGY, SNAPPER, POMFRET AND TREVALLY. SERVE THE FISH WITH FRIED RICE AND STIR-FRIED CHINESE GREEN VEGETABLES, SUCH AS PAK CHOI, IF YOU LIKE.

SERVES FOUR

INGREDIENTS

1 sea bass, about 1.4–1.5kg/
   3–3½lb, scaled and cleaned
8 spring onions (scallions)
60ml/4 tbsp teriyaki marinade or
   dark soy sauce
30ml/2 tbsp cornflour (cornstarch)
juice of 1 lemon
30ml/2 tbsp rice wine vinegar
5ml/1 tsp ground ginger
60ml/4 tbsp groundnut (peanut) oil
2 leeks, shredded
2.5cm/1in piece fresh root ginger,
   peeled and grated
105ml/7 tbsp chicken or fish stock
30ml/2 tbsp rice wine or dry sherry
5ml/1 tsp caster (superfine) sugar
salt and ground black pepper

1 Make several diagonal slashes on either side of the sea bass so it can absorb the flavours, then season the fish inside and out with salt and ground black pepper. Trim the spring onions, cut them in half lengthways, then slice them diagonally into 2cm/¾in lengths. Put half of the spring onions in the cavity of the fish and reserve the rest for later use.

2 In a shallow dish, mix together the teriyaki marinade or dark soy sauce, the cornflour, lemon juice, rice wine vinegar and ground ginger to make a smooth, runny paste. Turn the fish in the marinade to coat it thoroughly, working it into the slashes, then leave it to marinate for 20–30 minutes, turning it several times.

3 Heat a wok or frying pan that is large enough to hold the sea bass comfortably. Add the oil, then the leeks and grated ginger. Cook gently for about 5 minutes, until the leeks are tender. Remove the leeks and ginger with a slotted spoon and drain on kitchen paper. leaving the oil in the wok or pan.

4 Lift the sea bass out of the marinade and lower it carefully into the hot oil. Cook over a medium heat for 2–3 minutes on each side. Stir the stock, rice wine or sherry and sugar into the marinade, with salt and pepper to taste. Pour the mixture over the fish. Return the leeks and ginger to the wok, together with the reserved spring onions. Cover and simmer for about 15 minutes, until the fish is cooked through. Serve.

GRILLED LANGOUSTINES WITH HERBS

THIS SIMPLE COOKING METHOD ENHANCES BOTH THE DELICATE COLOUR AND FLAVOUR OF THE LANGOUSTINES. TRY TO FIND LIVE LANGOUSTINES FOR THIS RECIPE. CHOOSE THE LARGEST YOU CAN FIND (OR AFFORD) FOR THIS DISH, AND ALLOW 5–6 PER SERVING. LOBSTER AND CRAYFISH ARE ALSO DELICIOUS COOKED THIS WAY.

SERVES FOUR AS A MAIN COURSE,
SIX AS A STARTER

INGREDIENTS
    60ml/4 tbsp extra virgin olive oil
    60ml/4 tbsp hazelnut oil
    15ml/1 tbsp each finely chopped
      fresh basil, chives, chervil, parsley
      and tarragon
    pinch of ground ginger
    20–24 large langoustines,
      preferably live
    lemon wedges and rocket (arugula)
      leaves, to garnish
    salt and ground black pepper

COOK'S TIPS
• Don't forget to provide your guests with fingerbowls of warm water and plenty of paper napkins.
• If you use cooked langoustines, then grill (broil) them for just 2–3 minutes to warm them through.

1 Preheat the grill (broiler) to very hot. Mix together the olive and hazelnut oils in a small bowl. Add the herbs, a pinch of ground ginger and salt and pepper to taste. Whisk thoroughly until slightly thickened and emulsified.

2 If you are using live langoustines, immerse them in a pan of boiling water for 1–2 minutes, then drain and leave them to cool.

3 Split the langoustines lengthways using a large sharp knife and arrange them on a foil-lined grill pan. Spoon over the herb-flavoured oil.

4 Grill (broil) for 8–10 minutes, basting the langoustines two or three times until they are cooked and lightly browned.

5 Arrange the langoustines on a warmed serving dish, pour the juices from the grill pan over and serve immediately garnished with lemon wedges and rocket leaves.

SEA BASS IN A SALT CRUST

BAKING FISH IN A CRUST OF SEA SALT ENHANCES THE FLAVOUR AND BRINGS OUT THE TASTE OF THE SEA. ANY FIRM FISH CAN BE COOKED IN THIS WAY. BREAK OPEN THE CRUST AT THE TABLE TO RELEASE THE GLORIOUS AROMA.

SERVES FOUR

INGREDIENTS
    1 sea bass, about 1kg/2¼lb, cleaned
      and scaled
    1 sprig each of fresh fennel,
      rosemary and thyme
    2kg/4½lb/13½ cups coarse sea salt
    mixed peppercorns
    seaweed or samphire, blanched, and
      lemon slices, to garnish

1 Preheat the oven to 240°C/475°F/ Gas 9. Fill the cavity of the sea bass with all the herbs and grind over some of the mixed peppercorns.

2 Spread half the salt on a shallow baking tray (ideally oval) and lay the sea bass on it. Cover the fish all over with a 1cm/½in layer of salt, pressing it down firmly. Moisten the salt lightly by spraying with water from an atomizer. Bake the fish in the hot oven for 30–40 minutes, until the salt crust is just beginning to colour.

3 Garnish the baking tray with seaweed or samphire and bring the fish to the table in its salt crust. Use a sharp knife to break open the crust. Serve the fish, adding lemon slices to each plate.

FILLETS OF BRILL IN RED WINE SAUCE

FORGET THE OLD MAXIM THAT RED WINE AND FISH DO NOT GO WELL TOGETHER. THE ROBUST SAUCE ADDS COLOUR AND RICHNESS TO THIS EXCELLENT DISH. TURBOT, HALIBUT AND JOHN DORY ARE ALSO GOOD COOKED THIS WAY.

SERVES FOUR

INGREDIENTS

4 fillets of brill, about
  175–200g/6–7oz each, skinned
150g/5oz/⅔ cup chilled butter,
  diced, plus extra for greasing
115g/4oz shallots, thinly sliced
200ml/7fl oz/scant 1 cup robust
  red wine
200ml/7fl oz/scant 1 cup fish stock
salt and ground white pepper
fresh chervil or flat leaf parsley
  leaves, to garnish

3 Using a fish slice (spatula), carefully lift the fish and shallots on to a serving dish, cover with foil and keep hot.

4 Transfer the casserole to the hob and bring the cooking liquid to the boil over a high heat. Cook it until it has reduced by half. Lower the heat and whisk in the chilled butter, one piece at a time, to make a smooth, shiny sauce. Season with salt and ground white pepper, set aside and keep hot.

5 Divide the shallots among four warmed plates and lay the brill fillets on top. Pour the sauce over and around the fish and garnish with the chervil or flat leaf parsley.

1 Preheat the oven to 180°C/350°F/ Gas 4. Season the fish on both sides with salt and pepper. Generously butter a flameproof dish, which is large enough to take all the brill fillets in a single layer without overlapping. Spread the shallots over the base and lay the fish fillets on top. Season.

2 Pour in the red wine and fish stock, cover the dish and bring the liquid to just below boiling point. Transfer to the oven and bake for 6–8 minutes, until the brill is just cooked.

BAKED SEA BREAM WITH TOMATOES

JOHN DORY, TURBOT OR SEA BASS CAN ALL BE COOKED THIS WAY. IF YOU PREFER TO USE FILLETED FISH, CHOOSE A CHUNKY FILLET, LIKE COD, AND ROAST IT SKIN-SIDE UP. ROASTING THE TOMATOES BRINGS OUT THEIR SWEETNESS, WHICH CONTRASTS BEAUTIFULLY WITH THE FLAVOUR OF THE FISH.

2 Meanwhile, cut the potatoes into 1cm/½in slices. Par-boil for 5 minutes. Drain and set aside.

3 Grease an ovenproof dish with oil. Arrange the potatoes in a single layer with the lemon slices over; sprinkle on the bay leaf, thyme and basil. Season and drizzle with half the remaining olive oil. Lay the fish on top, season; pour over the wine and the rest of the oil. Arrange the tomatoes around the fish.

SERVES FOUR TO SIX

INGREDIENTS
  8 ripe tomatoes
  10ml/2 tsp caster (superfine) sugar
  200ml/7fl oz/scant 1 cup olive oil
  450g/1lb new potatoes
  1 lemon, sliced
  1 bay leaf
  1 fresh thyme sprig
  8 fresh basil leaves
  1 sea bream or porgy, about 900g–1kg/
    2–2¼lb, cleaned and scaled
  150ml/¼ pint/⅔ cup dry white wine
  30ml/2 tbsp fresh white breadcrumbs
  2 garlic cloves, crushed
  15ml/1 tbsp finely chopped
    fresh parsley
  salt and ground black pepper
  fresh flat parsley or basil leaves,
    chopped, to garnish

1 Preheat the oven to 240°C/475°F/ Gas 9. Cut the tomatoes in half lengthways and arrange them in a single layer in an ovenproof dish, cut-side up. Sprinkle with sugar, salt and pepper and drizzle over a little of the olive oil. Roast for 30–40 minutes, until soft and lightly browned.

4 Mix together the breadcrumbs, garlic and parsley; sprinkle over the fish. Bake for 30 minutes, until the flesh comes away easily from the bone. Garnish with chopped parsley or basil.

FILLETS OF SEA BREAM IN FILO PASTRY

ANY FIRM FISH FILLETS CAN BE USED FOR THIS DISH — BASS, GROUPER, RED MULLET AND SNAPPER ARE PARTICULARLY GOOD. EACH LITTLE PARCEL IS A MEAL IN ITSELF AND CAN BE PREPARED SEVERAL HOURS IN ADVANCE, WHICH MAKES THIS AN IDEAL RECIPE FOR ENTERTAINING. IF YOU LIKE, SERVE THE PASTRIES WITH FENNEL BRAISED WITH ORANGE JUICE OR A MIXED LEAF SALAD.

2 Thinly slice the potatoes lengthways. Brush a baking sheet with a little of the oil. Lay a sheet of filo pastry on the sheet, brush it with oil, then lay a second sheet crossways over the first. Repeat with two more sheets. Arrange a quarter of the sliced potatoes in the centre, season and add a quarter of the shredded sorrel or spinach. Lay a fish fillet on top, skin-side up. Season.

3 Loosely fold the filo pastry up and over to make a neat parcel. Make three more parcels; place on the baking sheet. Brush with half the butter. Bake for about 20 minutes, until the filo is puffed up and golden brown.

SERVES FOUR

INGREDIENTS

8 small waxy salad potatoes, preferably red-skinned
200g/7oz sorrel or spinach, stalks removed
30ml/2 tbsp olive oil
16 filo pastry sheets, thawed if frozen
4 sea bream or porgy fillets, about 175g/6oz each, scaled but not skinned
50g/2oz/¼ cup butter, melted
120ml/4fl oz/½ cup fish stock
250ml/8fl oz/1 cup whipping cream
salt and ground black pepper
finely diced red (bell) pepper, to garnish

1 Preheat the oven to 200°C/400°F/ Gas 6. Cook the potatoes in a pan of lightly salted boiling water for about 15–20 minutes, until just tender. Drain and leave to cool. Set about half the sorrel or spinach leaves aside. Shred the remaining leaves by piling up six at a time, rolling them up like a fat cigar and slicing them with a sharp knife.

4 Meanwhile, make the sorrel sauce. Heat the remaining butter in a pan, add the reserved sorrel and cook gently for 3 minutes, stirring, until it wilts. Stir in the stock and cream. Heat almost to boiling point, stirring so that the sorrel breaks down. Season to taste and keep hot until the fish parcels are ready. Serve garnished with red pepper. Hand round the sauce separately.

OCTOPUS STEW

THIS RUSTIC STEW IS A PERFECT DISH FOR ENTERTAINING, AS IT TASTES EVEN BETTER IF MADE A DAY IN ADVANCE. SERVE WITH A COLOURFUL SALAD OF BABY CHARD, ROCKET AND RADICCHIO.

SERVES FOUR TO SIX

INGREDIENTS

1kg/2¼lb octopus, cleaned
45ml/3 tbsp olive oil
1 large red onion, chopped
3 garlic cloves, finely chopped
30ml/2 tbsp brandy
300ml/½ pint/1¼ cups dry white wine
800g/1¾lb ripe plum tomatoes,
  peeled and chopped, or two
  400g/14oz cans chopped tomatoes
1 fresh red chilli, seeded and
  chopped (optional)
450g/1lb small new potatoes
15ml/1 tbsp chopped fresh rosemary
15ml/1 tbsp fresh thyme leaves
1.2 litres/2 pints/5 cups fish stock
30ml/2 tbsp fresh flat leaf
  parsley leaves
salt and ground black pepper
rosemary sprigs, to garnish
For the garlic croûtes
  1 fat garlic clove, peeled
  8 thick slices of baguette or
    ciabatta bread
  30ml/2 tbsp olive oil

3 Pour the brandy over the octopus and ignite it. When the flames have died down, add the wine, bring to the boil and bubble gently for about 5 minutes. Stir in the tomatoes, with the chilli, if using, then add the potatoes, rosemary and thyme. Simmer for 5 minutes.

4 Pour in the fish stock and season well. Cover the pan and simmer for 20–30 minutes, stirring occasionally. The octopus and potatoes should be very tender and the sauce should have thickened slightly. At this stage, you can leave the stew to cool, then put it in the refrigerator overnight.

5 Preheat a medium-hot grill (broiler). To make the croûtes, cut the garlic clove in half and rub both sides of the slices of bread with the cut side. Crush the garlic, stir it into the oil and brush the mixture over both sides of the bread. Grill (broil) on both sides until the croûtes are golden brown and crisp.

6 To serve the stew, reheat it gently if it has been in the refrigerator overnight, check the seasoning and stir in the parsley leaves. Serve piping hot in individual warmed bowls, garnished with rosemary sprigs and accompanied by the warm garlic croûtes.

1 Cut the octopus into large pieces, put these in a pan and pour in cold water to cover. Season with salt, bring to the boil, then lower the heat and simmer for 30 minutes to tenderize. Drain and cut into bitesize pieces.

2 Heat the oil in a large shallow pan. Cook the onion for 2–3 minutes, until lightly coloured, then add the garlic and cook for 1 minute. Add the octopus and cook for 2–3 minutes, stirring and tossing to colour it lightly on all sides.

FILLETS OF TURBOT WITH OYSTERS

This luxurious dish is perfect for special occasions. It is worth buying a whole turbot and asking the fishmonger to fillet and skin it for you. Keep the head, bones and trimmings for stock. Sole, brill and halibut can all be substituted for the turbot.

SERVES FOUR

INGREDIENTS

12 Pacific (rock) oysters
115g/4oz/½ cup butter
2 carrots, cut into julienne strips
200g/7oz celeriac, cut into julienne strips
the white parts of 2 leeks, cut into julienne strips
375ml/13fl oz/generous 1½ cups Champagne or dry white sparkling wine (about ½ bottle)
105ml/7 tbsp whipping cream
1 turbot, about 1.75kg/4–4½lb, filleted and skinned
salt and ground white pepper

1 Using an oyster knife, open the oysters over a bowl to catch the juices, then carefully remove them from their shells, discarding the shells, and place them in a separate bowl. Set aside until required.

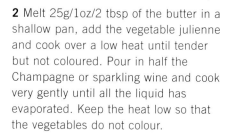

2 Melt 25g/1oz/2 tbsp of the butter in a shallow pan, add the vegetable julienne and cook over a low heat until tender but not coloured. Pour in half the Champagne or sparkling wine and cook very gently until all the liquid has evaporated. Keep the heat low so that the vegetables do not colour.

3 Strain the oyster juices into a small pan and add the cream and the remaining Champagne or sparkling wine. Place over a medium heat until the mixture has reduced to the consistency of thin cream. Dice half the remaining butter and whisk it into the sauce, one piece at a time, until smooth. Season to taste, then pour the sauce into a blender and process until velvety smooth.

4 Return the sauce to the pan, bring it to just below boiling point, then drop in the oysters. Poach for about 1 minute, to warm but barely cook. Keep warm, but do not let the sauce boil.

5 Season the turbot fillets with salt and pepper. Heat the remaining butter in a large frying pan until foaming, then cook the fillets over a medium heat for about 2–3 minutes on each side until cooked through and golden.

6 Cut each turbot fillet into three pieces and arrange on individual warmed plates. Pile the vegetable julienne on top, place three oysters around the turbot fillets on each plate and pour the sauce around the edge.

VEGETABLE-STUFFED SQUID

SHIRLEY CONRAN FAMOUSLY SAID THAT LIFE IS TOO SHORT TO STUFF A MUSHROOM. THE SAME MIGHT BE SAID OF SQUID, EXCEPT THAT THE RESULT IS SO DELICIOUS THAT IT MAKES THE EFFORT SEEM WORTHWHILE. SMALL CUTTLEFISH CAN BE PREPARED IN THE SAME WAY. SERVE WITH SAFFRON RICE.

SERVES FOUR

INGREDIENTS

4 medium squid, or 12 small squid,
  skinned and cleaned
75g/3oz/6 tbsp butter
50g/2oz/1 cup fresh
  white breadcrumbs
2 shallots, chopped
4 garlic cloves, chopped
1 leek, finely diced
2 carrots, finely diced
150ml/¼ pint/⅔ cup fish stock
30ml/2 tbsp olive oil
30ml/2 tbsp chopped fresh parsley
salt and ground black pepper
rosemary sprigs, to garnish
saffron rice, to serve

1 Preheat the oven to 220°C/425°F/ Gas 7. Cut off the tentacles and side flaps from the squid and chop these finely. Set the squid aside. Melt half the butter in a large frying pan that can safely be used in the oven. Add the fresh white breadcrumbs and fry until they are golden brown, stirring to prevent them from burning. Using a slotted spoon, transfer the breadcrumbs to a bowl and set aside until required.

2 Heat the remaining butter in the frying pan and add the chopped and diced vegetables. Fry until softened but not browned, then stir in the fish stock and cook until the stock has reduced and the vegetables are very soft. Season to taste with salt and ground black pepper and transfer to the bowl with the breadcrumbs. Mix lightly together.

3 Heat half the olive oil in the frying pan, add the chopped squid and cook over a high heat for 1 minute. Remove the squid with a slotted spoon; stir into the vegetable mixture. Stir in the parsley.

4 Put the stuffing mixture into a piping (pastry) bag, or use a teaspoon to stuff the squid tubes with the mixture. Do not overfill them, as the stuffing will swell slightly during cooking. Secure the openings with cocktail sticks or toothpicks, or sew up with fine kitchen thread.

5 Heat the remaining olive oil in the frying pan, place the stuffed squid in the pan and cook until they are sealed on all sides and golden brown. Transfer the frying pan to the oven and roast the squid for 20 minutes.

6 Unless the squid are very small, carefully cut them into 3 or 4 slices and arrange on a bed of saffron rice. Spoon the cooking juices over and around the squid and serve immediately, with each serving garnished with sprigs of rosemary.

INDEX